C9999900011258

✓

CAREERS IN

COMPUTING AND IT

Second Edition

David Yardley

KOGAN PAGE

For Ben

First published in 1997
Second edition 2000

Kogan Page Limited
120 Pentonville Road
London N1 9JN

© Kogan Page, 1997, 2000

British Library Cataloguing in Publication Data

A CIP record for this book is available from the British Library.

ISBN 0 7494 3200 4

Typeset by Kogan Page
Printed and bound in Great Britain by Clays Ltd, St Ives plc

Contents

Acknowledgements

For granting permission to reprint copyright material, I would like to thank *Computer Weekly*, *The Guardian* and *Management Today*.

The employer case studies within this book could not have been written without the help and support from the following organizations, who gave up a lot of their time to answer the torrent of questions I had prepared for them.

British Telecom
Cap Gemini
Eidos (in particular, Louise Short who offered an invaluable amount of advice and information)
IBM UK
Intel Ireland
Oracle
Pearson Publishing
The Post Office

Finally, I would like to thank my wife, Anne, for being around when the going got tough.

Introduction

Is this the job for you?

- ❏ Do I have an interest in computing and IT?
- ❏ Am I keen to join an industry that is one of the fastest growing in the world?
- ❏ Do I want to be in well-paid and relatively secure employment?
- ❏ Am I confident I can use computers already and want to find a good job in IT?
- ❏ Am I prepared to learn new skills to meet the changing demands on the IT profession?
- ❏ Do I have a flexible and professional approach to work?
- ❏ Do I want to design or write computer systems, provide support or sell computer products?
- ❏ Do I have the motivation to start a new career in IT?

The impact of computing and information technology

The Internet revolution will have as great an impact on society as the industrial revolution in only a third of the time.

The *Guardian*, 16 June 1999

There can be few people today who have not witnessed the way computing and information technology (IT) has changed our lives. No longer do we use IT only within science and industry; we now use it for entertainment and personal development as well. With the home-PC market fully established we can now access huge amounts of information, which can help us in just about every aspect of life: from learning a new language to managing our personal finances.

This is great news if you are planning a career in IT, whether you are finding your first steps on the job ladder or planning a change of career. Today's IT industry is an exciting place to work – the number of opportunities available continues to rise and average salaries remain relatively high. Despite a small decrease in vacancies during the latter part of 1999, the industry is still experiencing a skills shortage – there are not enough *skilled* people to satisfy the number of job vacancies. Whilst there are many opportunities for experienced programmers and analysts, movement into these positions must be balanced by recruitment at junior levels to maintain the appropriate levels of skill within an organization.

There is no better time than now to consider a career in computing and information technology. It enjoys a high profile on TV and in the newspapers; and the Careers Service and major employers are working together to train people for careers within the industry. Similarly, there are now many more opportunities to study computing and information technology at colleges and universities. If *you* want a career in computing and information technology, then you should congratulate yourself on having already taken the first (and most important!) step – reading this book.

How to use this book

This book will give you an up-to-date insight into computing and information technology: how it has developed into the lucrative and rewarding industry it is today and how it will develop in the future. The early chapters of the book will provide you with general information on the IT industry: its structure, the jobs available and how you should set out to achieve your goal: a career in computing and information technology. Included in the book are a number of company profiles, which examine some of the major employers within the industry and case studies of their employees. These case studies relate to real people working in the IT industry, and describe what IT employees *really* do at work, how they got there and what *you* need to do if you want to work in a similar role.

The latter chapters of the book provide information on the qualifications and training opportunities available and where you can study for them.

This book can only provide a general guide to the many opportunities available for training and employment within the IT industry. If you follow the advice within it, however, you will be able to use your time well in planning a career in IT. Whatever you plan to do, be confident – plan for success!

2 What is computing and information technology?

Today we live in a society where we have access to an enormous amount of information from all over the world. In fact, there are very few places on the planet where information *cannot* be accessed. Such is the nature of this new society that governments throughout the world are already calling it the 'information society'.

The information society

'Information society' is a term often used to describe a society where IT and communication systems are combined to allow information to be collected and accessed throughout the world. This has finally been made possible because the IT industry, the telecommunications industry and the entertainment industry have shared their knowledge and resources to produce new 'information businesses'. Using the Internet, we can now access our bank accounts using our PC at home; we can shop electronically without visiting the supermarket; we can even sell our houses without using an estate agent.

What is the Internet?

'Internet' was a term originally used to describe a communications network that would continue to operate in the event of a nuclear war. Today, however, it is used to describe a massive network of computers linked throughout the world. The word literally means 'network of networks', as it comprises thousands of smaller national and local networks scattered throughout the world. On any given day the Internet connects about 15 million users in over 50 countries. In the UK alone, more than 11 million people use the Internet, and 10,000 new people request access to it every day.

The World Wide Web (often called the 'Web' or abbreviated to 'www') is often mentioned in relation to the Internet, but it is not the same. The Web is a way of providing universal access to huge amounts of information, which can be text (documents), sound or images. The Internet, however, is the physical side of the global network (the giant mass of cables and computers, in other words).

The Internet revolution has created a new wave of opportunities for careers in computing and IT. At the time of writing, there were over 100 million Internet users, and this number is expected to increase to well over 700 million during the next decade. There has never been a technology that has brought together computers, networks and people in such a massive way as the Internet and, whatever you may think about it, the Internet (and all of the buzzwords associated with it) is here to stay. It wasn't so long ago that we heard phrases such as 'teletext', 'automatic teller machines' and 'floppy disks' for the first time; now we are hearing phrases such as 'e-shopping', 'cybercafés' and 'virtual bookshops'. The information society, however, is not just about the Internet; it is about *information*. Don't forget, almost 80 per cent of the world's population has never even used a telephone, let alone sent an e-mail message – we've got a long way to go.

What's in it for me?

Computing and IT is now used in just about every walk of life, from the demanding worlds of science, medicine, defence, politics and business to the more relaxing ones of recreation, entertainment and personal development. Figure 2.1 shows where and how computing and IT can be used – it is by no means the complete picture, but it should help in deciding your route into computing and IT.

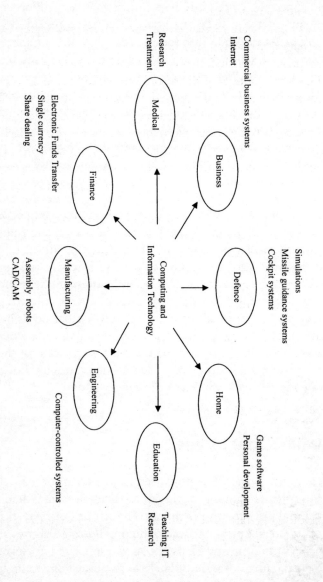

Figure 2.1 The many uses of computing and IT

There is no better time to think about a career in computing and information technology. IT is rarely out of the headlines, but there's no point in hearing how good something is if you cannot become a part of it.

IT issues are regularly discussed in the 'Bill Gates Column' of *Management Today* magazine. Hot topics in this column have (not surprisingly) included how others can match the success of Bill Gates (the founder of Microsoft) himself. Whilst he admits it may no longer be easy to build another Microsoft, in the June 1999 issue he does offer the following advice: 'I won't say you can build another Microsoft, but you can shoot for $2 million a year in sales by selling 10,000 copies of a $200 product.' His column goes on to discourage the reader from writing another word processor, spreadsheet or other product that has strong competition in the market, suggesting instead that he or she should 'create a product that helps people to do something specific or gives practical information in areas such as medicine, accounting, architecture or government processes. Software like this will make many small fortunes.'

During 1999, a schoolboy aged 17 had the Web site he had developed valued at over £3.1 million after being in business for just seven months. Benjamin Cohen's site (www.jewishnet.co.uk) had over 2 million visitors and quickly attracted the attentions of big business. His idea was simple: to link the Jewish community with Jewish business – a *Yellow Pages* in essence. It can be done!

The IT skills shortage

There have always been skills shortages in IT and there have always been people who complain they cannot get a job. Whilst this is probably true for all professions, the IT profession *is* different. IT is changing at an alarmingly fast rate and, just as those in traditional crafts had to change to keep up with the times, so too must today's IT professionals. Luckily, however, technology outpaces the acquisition of new skills by sufficient numbers of people to meet demand, so there should always be a skills shortage in certain IT disciplines. If you're not sure which area of IT to enter, you might want to consider gaining skills in one or more of the categories shown in Table 2.1 – for several years people with skills in these categories have remained in demand.

Table 2.1   IT skills most in demand

Position (Apr–Jun 1999)	Position (Apr–Jun 1998)	Skill	Category
1	4	Oracle	relational database
2	1	Windows NT	PC operating system
3	2	C++	programming language
4	3	Unix	operating system
5	5	Visual Basic	programming language
6	7	SQL	database query language
7	6	C	programming language
8	8	COBOL	programming language for large computer systems
9	9	Windows	PC operating system
10	11	Java	object-oriented programming language

(*Source:* SSP/*Computer Weekly* Quarterly Survey of Appointments Data and Trends)

In *Skills 99*, a report presented to the Department for Education and Employment, two key concerns were raised about the IT industry: the lack of skills in IT professionals and the lack of IT professionals. The first concern was about the *skills gap*, which can be tackled through better training and planning; the latter was about the true skills shortage, that is, the actual *lack of people*. A similar report, commissioned by Microsoft in association with the Computer Services and Software Association (CSSA) and the National Training Organization for IT (ITNTO), concluded that 75 per cent of the people questioned thought there was an IT skills shortage, a figure that rose to 90 per cent for those working in the finance sector.

Although the number of people in the IT profession has increased by 10 per cent in the last few years, the number of people with the *right* skills for the job is falling. For anyone wanting a career in computing and IT, this does offer some hope – if you can obtain the right skills for the jobs most in demand, you will have a much better chance of gaining employment.

Flexibility is the key however. IT *is* changing and so is business; to enter the IT world and enjoy a successful and rewarding career, you need to be flexible. Experience has shown that the area in which you start your IT career bears little resemblance to the area in which you end up. The IT industry is about computers, but it is also about *people*. Having a flexible attitude to where you work and what you do can often mean the difference between success and failure. Whilst there will always be a need for specialists in the industry, if you possess skills that are in demand in more than one industry sector, you should have a fairly secure and rewarding career. Table 2.2 should give you an idea of the main areas within IT where you could work.

Table 2.2 Breakdown of IT jobs advertised by industry sector

Sector	Jobs in Apr–Jun 1999	Jobs in Apr–Jun 1998
Computer vendors	882	1,120
Software houses	19,279	24,124
Communication companies	3,431	3,227
Banking/finance	6,531	9,340
Distribution/retail	2,491	3,078
Media/publishing	739	1,091
Manufacturing	743	1,201
Engineering	1,013	1,660
Utilities/energy	344	517
Public sector	875	1,447

(*Source:* SSP/*Computer Weekly* Quarterly Survey of Appointments Data and Trends)

The imbalance between supply and demand is forcing advertisers to increase the salaries on offer for the many IT positions. Despite a gradual rise in inflation, IT salaries are still above the underlying rate. Table 2.3 should give you a good idea of what sort of salaries to expect in the main job areas within IT. Don't forget, these figures are based on the 'transfer value' of existing, experienced IT professionals; the starting salaries for a first job are considerably lower. Having said that, there are many London-based IT consultancy companies that are more than willing to pay over £20,000 to attract graduates in any discipline into their own training and development programme.

Table 2.3   Average IT salaries on offer during 1999

Job title	Average salary offered in Apr–Jun 1999	Average salary offered in Apr–Jun 1998	Change
Management/ systems consultant	£72,485	£73,269	-1%
IT manager	£54,039	£50,893	+6%
Systems analyst	£28,247	£27,277	+4%
Programmer	£23,212	£22,217	+4%
Analyst programmer	£26,913	£25,489	+6%
Systems developer	£31,349	£30,157	+4%

(*Source:* SSP/*Computer Weekly* Quarterly Survey of Appointments Data and Trends)

Is a professional qualification really necessary?

The IT world remains undecided on what makes the best employees. Degree students possess many skills that are still seen as important to many employers, such as team-working, communication and problem-solving. Degrees also provide students with many general IT skills, allowing them to be more employable within different IT disciplines.

However, articles still appear regularly in the computer press from IT directors stating they do *not* want graduates. Being under pressure from business to deliver *immediate* benefits, they need people who can 'hit the ground running', ie they want people with skills they can use immediately, such as Visual Basic programmers or Microsoft NT administrators. As graduates often possess more academic skills (as opposed to vocational skills), companies must spend time retraining them in the key skills they need before they can be of any use.

Entering the IT industry with just programming skills (through a certified Microsoft training programme, for example) *will* provide you with much-needed skills in the short term, but you might suffer from a lack of awareness in many other areas you might need later on in your career, such as systems analysis, project management or financial analysis.

Computer science has now overtaken law to become the second most popular degree subject in the UK. During 1999, applications for entry into IT courses increased by 21 per cent. Compared with other professions, such as teaching, the attraction of high graduate starting salaries is certainly proving difficult to resist for many students. A survey of nearly 3,000 graduate jobs found average salaries had risen by nearly 9 per cent, more than six times the rate of inflation. Information technology jobs accounted for one in five of those on offer, and paid the second highest salaries (second to the management consultancies) at £17,254.

Whilst the number of graduates entering the profession continues to increase, it is worth noting that three-quarters of them do not have IT-related degrees and, according to some employers, this is no bad thing. For instance, the IT training manager at one of the largest financial services providers in the UK recently went on record to say that her company *preferred* to recruit non-IT graduates, as they came with no preconceived ideas about IT. Her staff train about 40 new recruits every year; fewer than half of them have IT degrees.

What *is* important, though, is that the computer industry is short of people with *skills*, not academic qualifications. Whilst gaining an academic qualification is one possible way of gaining IT skills, it is not the only way; there are numerous opportunities available today for people to gain the skills they need to get a job within IT. One thing is clear: once you have gained even a small amount of experience, the emphasis placed on academic qualifications reduces.

A brief history of computing and information technology

Computing and IT is breaking new technological barriers all the time, but it is nothing new. The first computers were developed during the 1940s, following years of research in both the UK and USA.

Early commercial computers were so large that one often filled an entire room; they also consumed huge amounts of power, and were very expensive to build. So great was the investment required that many experts believed only a few dozen would *ever* be needed.

With the development of the transistor, computers, still relatively expensive, began to take up less room and consume less power. Soon after came the development of the integrated circuit, which allowed thousands of transistors and other electrical components to be 'printed' on to a piece of silicon – the 'silicon chip', as we know it today. Mass production and sophisticated manufacturing techniques have since allowed the silicon chip to be produced in large numbers at little cost. Today, almost all electronic equipment, from a small camera to the largest commercial computer system, contains a 'microchip'.

3 Careers in computing and information technology

Since the advent of commercial computing in the 1960s, the IT industry has experienced many changes. If you are serious about working in the industry, you need to be aware of these changes. For many people, the lure of high salaries has obscured sensible judgement, causing many unnecessary career disappointments. Technology is changing all the time, and if you jump in headfirst, you are likely to end up being saddled with unmarketable skills in a mundane job rather than gaining new skills in the latest technologies. With a bit of thought and planning, this unfortunate situation can be easily avoided.

Understanding the main types of computers

When you start looking for employment within the IT industry, you will soon discover that some jobs are specific to a particular type of computer – the computer 'platform', as it is called. The main computer platforms you need to be aware of are super-computers, mainframe, mid-range and desktop, which are covered in the following sections.

Super-computers

Often restricted to large-scale research and development work, super-computers are extremely powerful and can process huge amounts of information (such as complex mathematical calculations) in a relatively short space of time, a process known as 'number-crunching'.

Super-computers are generally used for specific applications where the average computer would not be able to cope with the workload, such as processing weather information and performing complex 'virtual-reality' simulations (war-games, flight simulators, geographical models and so on). Despite being one of the most powerful computers on the planet, an IBM super-computer has only recently managed to beat a grandmaster in a well-publicized chess match, which goes to show the human brain is still the most powerful and complex computer of them all! The Cray computer is a popular model of super-computer.

Mainframe computers

Historically, commercial computing applications were developed using large computers called 'mainframes'. Today, mainframes are used in organizations that require large amounts of processing power and disk storage to perform the work required by the business. Company payroll, stock control and order-processing systems are just some of the applications found in mainframe computing. The IBM 3/90 range contains many popular models of mainframe computer.

Mid-range computers

Large business departments often use medium-sized computers or 'mini-computers', solely for one or two important business systems, such as order-processing and warehousing systems. Mid-range computing is becoming much more important in the IT industry, as high-performance systems are now being produced that directly compete with their more expensive mainframe neighbours. The IBM AS/400 range provides good examples of mid-range computers.

Desktop computers

PCs are now an everyday commodity owing to their enormous versatility and ease of use. The low price-tag coupled with relatively high performance has meant that their growth has been unstoppable. With software vendors, such as Microsoft, providing numerous applications for the PC, there seems little doubt that the desktop revolution is here to stay. Most PC systems in use today are based around the following operating systems: Windows 95, NT and Windows 2000.

The rise in client-server computing

From the earliest days of computing up until the 1980s, the traditional view of the computer system was based on the 'mainframe' computer. The mainframe was generally a large, powerful computer, often the size of a small car, housed in its own room – the computer building. It was on this type of computer system that *all* of the business applications were run, such as payroll systems, accounts and order-processing systems.

As it was the only computer within an organization, its users accessed it from visual display units (VDUs) or 'dumb terminals'. VDUs could only send and receive data to and from the mainframe computer as a stream of characters; the VDU had no processing power of its own to perform more complex functions, such as running programs and transferring data. The traditional mainframe-based system is illustrated in Figure 3.1.

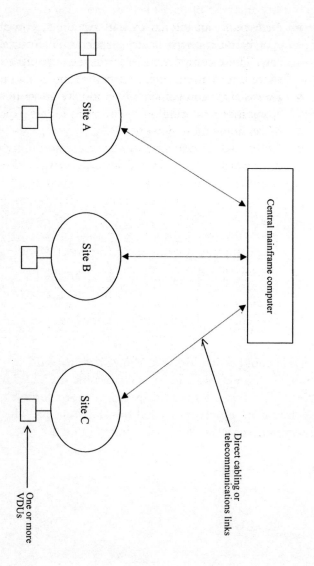

Figure 3.1 The traditional mainframe-based business system

Because of demand, market forces and new trends in IT, this traditional view of computer systems has changed. Over the last 20 years, the most noticeable changes have been:

♦ *Networking*: an interconnected system of computers that can share peripheral devices (such as tape units and printers). These computers can access data simultaneously and share information, such as data files and e-mail messages.

♦ *Downsizing*: companies are gradually moving expensive applications running on mainframes to less expensive but increasingly more powerful PCs.

♦ *Client-server computing*: a model of computing where computing tasks are distributed across a network as opposed to running on one central computer, such as a mainframe. The desktop PC (or client) runs under its own power and provides a graphical user interface (GUI, pronounced 'gooey') allowing the user to request and analyse data easily. The computer sending the information (the server) stores the data and processes requests from the client PCs. Client-server systems are popular because they make more efficient use of a network and ensure that data-processing tasks are spread more evenly among computers in the organization. When computer systems share resources, using a combination of networking and client-server systems, they are often referred to as 'distributed client-server systems' (see Figure 3.2).

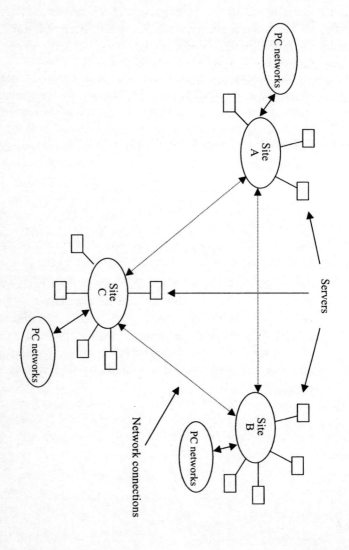

Figure 3.2 A typical distributed client–server system

The structure of the IT industry

The IT profession has, at its core, the software and hardware sectors that are fundamental in the development of all computer systems used today. However, as we have seen in earlier chapters, the information revolution has engulfed the telecommunication and entertainment industries to form new sectors within the IT profession. Whilst these new sectors are distinct from one another, there is nevertheless a high degree of interworking between them (see Figure 3.3).

Careers in software and computing services

Of all the areas within the IT industry, the software and services sector is the one that employs the most people and the one that can offer the most opportunities for first-time recruits. Its size and importance in terms of employment potential mean it is an area you should consider very carefully before deciding on any specific career path. It is estimated that more than 16,000 software and services companies, employing over 300,000 staff, exist in Western Europe alone. On top of this, additional employment is emerging with the development of the Internet and multi-media applications. Figure 3.4 gives an indication of the structure of the software and computing services sector within the European Union (EU).

Systems software
This area concerns the programs and utilities that control the computer and operate hardware. Collectively, they are referred to as the 'operating system'. As operating systems do not change substantially on a regular basis, the majority of work in the systems software sector is performed using specialist tools and programmes that help with:

◆ computer performance and tuning;
◆ database maintenance;
◆ archiving software to take backups of programs;
◆ security or 'access-control' software used to prevent unauthorized access to computer systems;
◆ diagnostic software used to detect network-related errors.

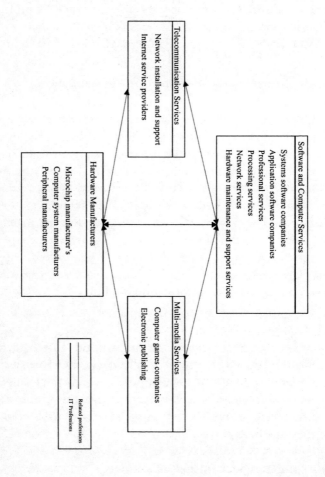

Figure 3.3 The structure of the IT industry

Software and Computer Services

Systems software companies
Application software companies
Professional services
Processing services
Network services
Hardware maintenance and support services

Telecommunication Services

Network installation and support
Internet service providers

Hardware Manufacturers

Microchip manufacturer's
Computer system manufacturers
Peripheral manufacturers

Multi-media Services

Computer games companies
Electronic publishing

Related professions
IT Professions

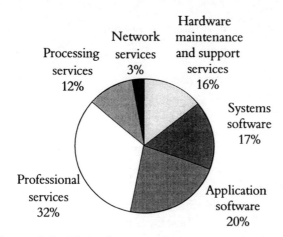

Figure 3.4 EU software and services market by segment
(*source:* EITO)

Whilst the majority of mainframes run IBM's MVS operating system, the systems software sector has flourished with the increase in UNIX and Microsoft NT, which run on PCs and small computer systems.

Applications software

Without application software, the most powerful computers in the world are of little use to anyone – it is software that provides business users with the applications they need to trade and compete successfully in the marketplace. The majority of this software provides business users with the capability to retrieve, manipulate and store business information quickly and easily (business people are not computer experts). Application software can be designed to run for one user on a PC, such as a database or word-processing package, or it can be designed to run for hundreds of users on large computer systems, where the application software might run the stock control system or the company's Web site.

Despite the PC revolution, the majority of application 'code' written is still designed to run on mainframe computers, mainly because they can store and process huge amounts of information extremely quickly, unlike most PCs.

Typical examples of application software used within business include:

- airline reservation systems;
- stock-control systems;
- financial accounts packages;
- word-processing, spreadsheet and database packages;
- Internet-based trading software.

Professional services

As the number of applications, technologies and strategies developed by the IT industry increases, so too does the number of options available to business, for instance: the computer platforms a business should use to develop or expand its IT capability; whether the business problem is big enough to warrant a very expensive mainframe or whether a few powerful PCs will do the same job; and how the business can take advantage of the Internet.

There are of course hundreds of other questions that organizations might ask (what software to buy is a popular one). None of these questions can be answered easily without understanding the organization's specific business requirements, both in the short term and in the long term (computer systems can become obsolete *very* quickly, so some thought must be taken when deciding what to buy).

IT services companies work closely with customers to identify their business requirements and the best ways of achieving them. Most companies in this sector, therefore, concentrate on providing some or all of the following: independent advice; designing; and developing and implementing IT requirements within an agreed budget and timescale.

Processing services

This category provides business with specific computing services, such as processing monthly payroll information. Bureau companies provide a useful service to organizations that do not wish to invest huge sums of money in computer systems for which they only have a limited use.

Software development in action

There is never a shortage of business problems requiring solutions using computer software, which is why a career within software development can be such an interesting one. When writing business software, it is crucial that you understand the needs and requirements of the business and are able to identify the technical solution necessary to solve the business problems. This is just the start of the lengthy process from business requirement to delivered computer solution – the 'system development life cycle' (see Figure 3.5).

Career prospects

There are very good opportunities for people wanting to work in the software and services sector. Programmers continue to remain in demand at all levels from junior programmers working for local government to software development consultants working for the large multinational companies. If you like programming or are technically minded, then a career working for the systems and application software companies seems an obvious choice. Consultancy companies, whilst requiring technical skills, must also employ people who can communicate and build a trusting relationship with the (fee-paying) customer.

If you want to walk straight into a consultancy role with one of the major professional service companies (eg Cap Gemini, EDS, Logica, IBM and ICL), you will without doubt need a good degree. Employers with graduate training programmes do not necessarily require degrees in a computing subject – they train you for whatever role you are best suited to.

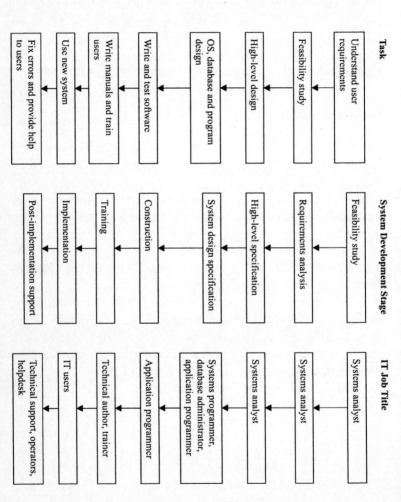

Task	System Development Stage	IT Job Title
Understand user requirements	Feasibility study	Systems analyst
Feasibility study	Requirements analysis	Systems analyst
High-level design	High-level specification	Systems analyst
OS, database and program design	System design specification	Systems programmer, database administrator, application programmer
Write and test software	Construction	Application programmer
Write manuals and train users	Training	Technical author, trainer
Use new system	Implementation	IT users
Fix errors and provide help to users	Post-implementation support	Technical support, operators, helpdesk

Figure 3.5   The system development life cycle and related IT jobs

Oracle Corporation

The Oracle Corporation is the world's largest supplier of database software and information management software, with annual revenues of over $4.2 billion. Oracle software, whilst often associated with UNIX systems, runs on almost every computer, from the smallest laptop to the massively powerful super-computers.

Oracle UK is a wholly owned subsidiary of the Oracle Corporation and employs over 4,500 people in 11 regional locations. Oracle UK has a European Porting Centre at Blackrock, Ireland from where it transfers (ports) its software on to different computer operating systems.

Career opportunities

Oracle UK recruits graduates from many different disciplines as well as computer science, so long as they have proven academic success in a relevant area. Normally only 10 per cent of applicants are invited for an interview, during which candidates are expected to sit psychometric tests. There is no formal recruitment policy, and students with A levels can apply for positions, as can school-leavers, normally as part of a youth training scheme.

Contact information

The best place to obtain information on Oracle and current career opportunities is its Web site: www.oracle.co.uk. Alternatively, contact Human Resources Department, Oracle UK Corporation Limited, Oracle Parkway, Thames Valley Park, Reading, Berkshire RG6 1RA (tel: 0118 924 0000).

Cap Gemini

Cap Gemini is the number one provider of consulting and IT services in Europe and the number three provider worldwide. It was founded over 20 years ago by the merger of three computer services and consulting companies: CAP, Gemini Computer Services and Sogeti.

The Cap Gemini Group provides a broad range of services, which can be organized into five main areas:

- consulting;
- project services;
- software products;
- information systems management;
- education and training.

Career opportunities

To work at a professional level within Cap Gemini you need a degree, although this can be in any subject. Candidates are expected to sit an aptitude test as part of the recruitment process.

Entry into this level is possible without a degree if candidates possess at least 18 months' experience in a particular IT field. As with many large companies, it provides entry-level opportunities for people who do not possess a degree. These are mainly based around providing a helpdesk support role for the desktop environment within the company (PCs, Windows, etc). Cap Gemini does not take people on straight from school.

Contact information

The best place to obtain information on Cap Gemini and current career opportunities is its Web site: www.capgemini.co.uk. Alternatively, contact Recruitment Services, CAP Gemini UK PLC, Cap Gemini House, 95 Wandsworth Road, London SW8 2HG (tel: 0171 735 0800).

Careers in hardware manufacturing

Despite the boom in software, computer hardware is still a substantial area within the IT industry. In 1993, the European computer market was estimated at £130 billion and growing. One-third of this total was spent with the hardware manufacturers.

During the early days of computing, the computer industry was dominated by a few huge companies (such as IBM and ICL), which were in fact hardware suppliers. The hardware market has changed significantly since then, and the IT industry has adopted a more 'open' approach. Customers are no longer forced to buy their computer hardware and software from the same manufacturer – they can go to any number of IT vendors. As a result, many hardware manufacturers now employ 'open' standards for chip design, computer interfaces and networking, allowing them to integrate their equipment with equipment from other manufacturers.

Who produces what?
Computers, regardless of shape, size or cost, rely upon silicon chips for their operation. As the demand for even more powerful computers increases, so too does the need for specialists capable of designing and manufacturing them. Almost 90 per cent of the high-performance chips found within large mid-range and mainframe computers are produced by Japanese-owned companies, such as Fujitsu and Mitsubishi, whilst the circuits found within most PCs are produced largely by US manufacturers such as Intel and Motorola.

It is worth remembering that careers in computer system manufacture involve a great deal more than just designing and testing integrated circuits. All computer systems are worthless unless there is some means of entering data into them and retrieving information from them. Every computer system therefore requires input and output devices, called peripherals, which include printers, display screens and storage devices (disks and tapes). There may also be networking and telecommunication equipment attached to the computer to allow information to be routed to another computer anywhere in the world. Computer peripherals are manufactured throughout the world, including in the UK and the rest of Europe.

Career prospects
Computer hardware manufacturers can offer many highly skilled careers, which cover every aspect of the manufacturing process from design to distribution. Whilst these companies seek to employ highly skilled professionals, there are always opportunities at more junior levels for people with fewer qualifications. It is often the case that a basic understanding of electronics and physics is all that is required for many of the entry-level opportunities within this area, as most if not all of the manufacturers have their own specific training and education programmes to develop expertise within the company. For example, IBM supports the NVQ programme, which provides on-the-job training and accreditation.

Qualifications

If you want to enter areas of computer manufacture such as microprocessor design and digital electronic technology at a professional level, you will normally require, at minimum, education to A level standard in subjects such as electronics, maths and computing. Even then, you will always face competition from those who have gained a degree in relevant subjects, such as computer science, digital electronics, and manufacturing and computing. Many of the larger computer manufacturers have extremely good graduate training programmes, and so can take on graduates in *any* discipline – yet more competition for those without a degree, unfortunately.

If you want to enter this field at an entry level, having a support and administration role as opposed to a design and construction role, you often need no more than a GCSE level of education. What is important at this level is having an *active* interest in computer design and manufacture, and the ability to learn new skills. For example, the following skills would be considered very useful for a junior position in computer design and manufacture:

◆   an interest in electronics, especially digital electronics;
◆   an interest in building, customizing and fixing computers;
◆   an understanding of 'low-level' computer programming;
◆   the ability to reason logically;
◆   good mathematical skills;
◆   the ability to understand and communicate technical issues effectively.

IBM UK

IBM UK is a subsidiary of the IBM Corporation, which is one of the world's largest suppliers of information technology hardware, software, solutions and services. IBM is truly a worldwide IT company, providing solutions to customers in over 130 countries. Within the UK, IBM has sites at more than 25 locations, including Basingstoke, Bedfont Lakes, Greenock, Hursley, London, Portsmouth, Manchester and Warwick.

IBM's main activities include:

- manufacturing;
- development and support for computer software and hardware;
- software and consultancy services;
- Internet development and electronic trading services.

All the manufacturing performed by IBM in the UK is performed at its Greenock site in Scotland. IBM employs more than 3,000 people at this site in a wide variety of manufacturing and technical roles ranging from high-volume assembly to IT management.

IBM Greenock is responsible for the development, manufacture and support of PCs for the European, Middle Eastern and African markets, and is the only site within IBM worldwide where design, manufacture and support are completely integrated. Already it employs over 250 overseas staff who manage the customer's order from manufacture to delivery. This is carried out for 76 countries in 17 different languages. One of the most popular IBM products, the award-winning IBM ThinkPad, is manufactured entirely at Greenock.

Qualifications required

IBM accepts graduates from many disciplines, ranging from scientific and computing areas to the arts. As you would expect from a company with such a wide range of career options, IBM can offer employment at all levels; and for the more technical positions, it welcomes graduates with masters degrees. Having operations throughout the world, it is particularly keen to recruit IT professionals with language skills as well as technical skills. IBM regularly advertises at recruitment fairs and exhibitions throughout the year.

Contact information

Contact Recruitment Services, PO Box 41, North Harbour, Portsmouth, Hants PO6 3AU.

Intel Ireland Ltd

Intel Ireland is a subsidiary of the massive Intel Corporation, one of the market leaders in microprocessor design and manufacture. It is one of the largest IT companies to invest in Ireland, with over $1 billion invested in its Ireland operation by the end of 1995.

Intel's manufacturing complex at County Kildare is the company's sole manufacturing centre for Europe, with four factories on site. The company directly employs over 2,800 people, with another 800 people being employed on site by other service companies.

Intel's main activities include:

- manufacture of semiconductor products (eg Pentium processor);
- manufacture of PC motherboards;
- manufacture of PCs and servers for leading computer vendors;
- PC maintenance and repair.

Qualifications required

Over a third of Intel employees are graduates. However, due to the wide-ranging skills used within the company, graduates are recruited from many disciplines, such as electronic engineering, mechanical engineering, computer science and information technology. As you would expect from a company whose operations are widespread, Intel can offer employment at all levels within the company; it recruits entry-level employees with a minimum of five passes on their Leaving Certificate (the Irish equivalent of A levels).

Intel readily accepts 'on-spec' CVs for current and future positions – these are scanned electronically and stored on its recruitment database. Should a vacancy exist (Intel is currently recruiting heavily), the database is searched and a shortlist drawn up.

Contact information

Contact Personnel Department, Collinstown Industrial Park, Leixlip, County Kildare, Ireland (tel: 00 353 1 606 7000).

4 Careers in multi-media

The electronic publishing industry

The electronic publishing industry is rapidly emerging as one of the most successful sectors within the information technology profession. With the almost seamless transition from floppy disk to CD ROM (compact disc read-only memory), and now to DVD (digital versatile disk), the products of this new 'multi-media' industry are now readily used both in the home and within business. For instance, over 100,000 copies of Microsoft's *Encarta* encyclopaedia were sold in the UK during 1994. Whilst this industry has many key players in the UK, the production of multi-media titles at present is clearly dominated by the USA.

Like many other 'new' industries that have emerged from the growth of the 'information society', electronic publishing has its roots firmly based around one very old industry – publishing. Whilst the key objectives of the publishing industry have changed little, the way in which they are now achieved using IT is considerably different to the techniques used 10 years ago.

The multi-media industry is a big user of expensive PC-based hardware and software; and just because publishing techniques have changed, the objectives are still the same – to make money by selling a quality product. To develop the product, (newspapers, books, videos and so on), often specialist IT hardware and software are necessary so the complex images required can be transposed on to a wide variety of media, such as paper, CD ROM, DVD and, of course, the Web.

The scope for rewarding careers in this fast-moving, demanding industry is great. IT skills are used alongside publishing skills to provide many varied roles and responsibilities. Publishing tasks involve writing, editing, proof-reading and design work. IT tasks involve supporting the hardware, software and networks, and writing 'in-house' software for publishing tasks or even producing encryption algorithms to protect information (such as electronic books and applications) distributed on CD ROM.

The main software packages used in the electronic publishing industry can be generally categorized as desktop publishing software and photo-imaging software.

Desktop publishing software is similar to word-processing software, but is used for editing and controlling multiple documents, such as the sections of a newspaper or chapters in a book. One of the most popular desktop publishing packages used in the industry is QuarkXPress.

Photo-imaging software is used for the images (pictures, photographs and diagrams, for example) found in books and newspapers, practically all of which are now produced electronically, using digital image-editing programs and scanners. Using these publishing tools, source images (such as photographs) can be 'scanned' into the computer and edited using specialist software. This software is similar to an art or graphics package that might be used in the home, allowing parts of the image to be edited. A good example of how this is used within the electronic publishing industry can be found in the front page of the 'glossy' fashion magazines. Photographs of models (especially close-up facial shots) are often 'touched up' so that they appear perfect. One of the most popular imaging and graphics packages used in the industry is Adobe Photoshop.

What qualifications will I need?

The qualifications you need largely depend on the level at which you wish to enter the industry. A degree in maths, physics or IT (with a passing interest in art and design!) allows you entry to the more senior levels of the industry. If, however, you prefer to enter the industry with 'real' skills rather than academic qualifications, you might want to consider courses offering vocational skills and training. Courses such as a GNVQ in art and design and computing will provide you with the basic skills you need.

Salaries
Average starting salaries can be between £15,000 and £17,000 a year. Top-level graduates (by Oxford and Cambridge standards) can expect £35,000–£40,000 straight from university (some London 'city' companies are even offering an £8,000 'golden handshake' for students accepting offers of employment.

Pearson Publishing

Pearson Publishing is a small group of businesses that produces high-quality educational products and services on various forms of electronic multi-media as well as on the traditional 'printed page'. In practice, this means the company not only produces materials on 'fixed' electronic media (such as CD ROM), but also on 'online' media (such as the Web).

Specializing in information and communications technology, its emphasis is on applying new technologies to the preparation of teaching, training and marketing materials.

Career opportunities

Being one of the smaller companies in this sector (not to be confused with the huge international multi-media company, Pearson plc), it needs highly motivated and bright people who can quickly become experts in all the major areas of multi-media publishing. Whilst publishing tasks such as design, editing and proof-reading are performed, these form only a part of the whole operation. Specific IT tasks such as building networks, writing in-house software, building demonstrations and supporting all the IT hardware and software are also performed.

Most of their employees are Cambridge graduates who have studied maths, physics or computing. However, the company does employ students who possess A levels (not necessarily in IT and computing, but it helps).

The computer games industry

Whilst there are computers available, there will always be computer games to play on them. Many PC owners only use their PCs for playing games. Compared to the offerings from today's computer games industry, the early Space Invaders arcade games now seem like child's play, but they did hook a generation of children and adults on to the concept of the computer game. This fact alone suggests that the computer games industry is huge – well it is, and that means that there are fantastic opportunities for careers in this rapidly expanding and exciting area. These opportunities are borne out by the growth in the UK for PC games: in 1997, the UK PC games industry grew by a whopping 85 per cent; worldwide, the computer games industry is now worth over \$6 billion!

Game console manufacturers

Originally, the entertainment industry concentrated mainly on audio entertainment, but over the years it changed, developing new technologies that combined information technology with new forms of audio-visual entertainment.

At the time of writing, the new 128-bit Sega Dreamcast console was launched in the UK amidst manufacturer's claims that it was the world's most powerful games console. At £199, the Dreamcast console provides connection to the Internet and the World Wide Web for a quarter of the price of the average PC. The Dreamcast, when launched in the USA during late 1999, clocked up 370,000 sales on its first day, suggesting that the demand for the latest games systems will always be high.

The Sony Corporation, with a long and successful history in the entertainment business, is a perfect example of how such changes can lead to great success. Following the huge success of its PlayStation games console, the PlayStation II will go on sale in 2000. Like the Sega Dreamcast, it too will come with an in-built modem, allowing it to connect to the Internet, providing (in theory at least) electronic mail capability and the ability to play games over 'cyberspace'. With Sony selling 50 million of the original

PlayStations worldwide in just five years, the games console can now be considered a popular computer system in its own right.

Games software companies

Mega-selling games such as Tomb Raider (despite what you might think) are not the product of one company; they are in fact the end product of a number of companies. This is no coincidence: a lot of specialist skills are needed for companies to produce a product that in many ways is the computer equivalent of a blockbuster Hollywood movie.

Companies such as Eidos (the company behind Tomb Raider) do not actually write computer games software, but provide an 'umbrella group' for a number of smaller companies that specialize in areas such as marketing, advertising, distribution and research. The actual design and programming aspects in the production of computer games are normally performed by small, independent software development studios, which are commissioned to supply computer games by the big umbrella companies, such as Eidos.

5 Telecommunications services

The telecommunications services sector covers the many areas surrounding the transmission of different types of signals, such as speech, data and images. Whilst most people might loosely call this 'networking', it is much more than that. It includes managing not only the building and running of the networks, but also the provision of services such as electronic commerce and electronic messaging systems.

Telecommunication companies

Many of the larger telecommunications companies operating today were originally established to provide and support the public telephone system or to provide telecommunications services to business. Today, little has changed, with the exception that all telecommunications companies can now compete in almost all markets. With the increased use of digital technologies and high-speed networks, the ability to reach these new markets has increased tremendously, and opportunities for employment are good.

With the convergence of IT and telecommunications, and the provision of services such as Internet-based trading (electronic commerce) and electronic mail, telecommunications companies are now major players in the IT industry. As well as developing new business areas using the Internet, telecommunications companies are leading the way in making available existing business technologies for home and personal use, such as mobile phone systems, fast ISDN (integrated services digital network) lines and remote video-conferencing systems.

Internet service providers

Any business operating a Web site, such as a high-street shop, a train company or a government department, must use telecommunications services to allow customers to access their information and services. Internet service providers (ISPs) provide such a service by allowing other companies and individuals access to their network for their own purposes, such as hosting a Web site and using electronic mail. However, not all ISPs are telecommunications companies; many of the popular ISPs (which now include many high-street supermarkets) use the network facilities owned by telecommunications companies such as BT, Energis and Mercury.

Whilst the number of ISPs seems to be growing all the time (during 1999 there were more than 100), all ISPs fall into one of two categories: online content providers and free Internet access providers. Online content providers (named because of the information or 'content' they offer) charge for their services in addition to the cost of the phone call. The second category contains those ISPs that provide free Internet access services (or free 'content'), but you still have to pay for the cost of the phone call.

BT plc

BT is one of the world's leading telecommunications companies, whose principal activity is the supply of local, long-distance and international telecommunications services and equipment in the UK. Employing over 100,000 people, it is one of the largest companies in Europe.

Recent trends in UK telecommunications, especially in mobile telecommunications and Internet traffic, have helped BT increase its turnover to over £18,233 million in 1999. Despite increased competition in the telecommunications sector, BT still looks after more than 20 million domestic UK customers and thousands of businesses.

Whilst most people recognize BT as the main provider of domestic telephone lines and digital business lines such as ISDN, BT is extremely successful in integrating telecommunications and IT technologies. This means it is able to diversify its business interests across many IT areas. Syntegra and Syncordia, BT's systems integration and outsourcing businesses, are prime examples of how complex IT and telecommunications technologies can be used and managed successfully. Syncordia Solutions, for example, is the UK's largest provider of managed and outsourced network solutions, and has more than 27,000 clients in 46 countries.

What opportunities are available?

As you might expect from a huge organization committed to employing high-calibre people, BT offers many exciting career prospects and is keen to promote and offer many exciting opportunities at all levels within the company.

Work experience

Each year BT welcomes around 3,000 students on its work experience scheme, which operates throughout all of its business areas. If you are at secondary school, you can gain work experience for either one or two weeks with BT. However, the responsibility for finding the placement lies with you. You can use any means available to help find a contact within BT, who can then register you with a BT manager for a work experience placement. Possible contacts might include:

- family;
- friends;
- neighbours;
- school contacts.

BT Modern Apprenticeship Scheme

To apply, you need to be:

- aged between 16 and 21 on 1 September 1999;
- a good communicator who enjoys helping people and solving problems;
- diligent and punctual in your work and training;
- not participating in any other government-funded training scheme;
- in possession of, or likely to achieve, at least five GCSEs at grade C or above (or equivalent), including English language and maths (Standard Grades 1 or 2 in Scotland);
- telecommunications and information technology apprentices also need grade C or above in combined science or physics.

Some vacancies require higher qualifications. BT also welcomes applications if you have some A levels.

Graduate recruitment

Graduates are seen as critical to the future success of BT, possessing up-to-date knowledge and skills. Whilst the number of graduates recruited dipped in 1993/4 to around 200, BT now has a graduate recruitment that is amongst the five largest in the UK.

For graduate opportunities, BT expect you to hold at least a good second-class honours degree in a relevant discipline (you must also have GCSE maths and English language at grade C or above – or equivalent qualifications).

What areas can I work in?

With a degree in computer science or information technology, opportunities exist in many business areas. A few of the key ones are:

- sales technical;
- research and development;
- Internet and multi-media applications;
- systems and software;
- project management.

Sandwich placements are available, as are student skills training workshops.

Contact details

Further details are available on BT's Web site:
www.bt.com/recruitment/graduate

6 Using computing and IT in business

Computing and IT is now used in practically every business organization worldwide. How it is used varies enormously – the local corner shop might possess a single computer terminal to process national lottery tickets whereas a large multinational company might invest millions in the latest IT and global communication systems so it can transfer data worldwide. Both types of organization, however, are using IT for the same reason: to improve their business, either by increasing revenue or by improving existing business functions (sometimes referred to as 'business process re-engineering'). These organizations (the IT users) form an important part of the IT community, as they are the people who decide whether or not to use the latest technology available. If they choose not to use such technology, preferring to stay with existing 'tried and tested' systems, many IT vendors risk losing vital sales.

Major IT users

Banking and finance

Since the introduction of the cash machine (or automatic teller machine), the banking and finance sector has probably seen the greatest level of change since the introduction of IT. By using the Internet to provide online banking and share-dealing services, this sector more than ever is now completely dependent on computing and IT. One major high-street bank alone, the National Westminster, in 1998 had more than 800 full-time and 300 part-time IT staff!

Retail

Many traditional forms of trading, such as shopping at the local supermarket, are now undergoing many changes. IT not only allows the supermarkets to operate more efficiently (and therefore make greater profits), but has also given them the capability to trade using new technologies such as the Internet and interactive TV.

Food is not the only retail sector to benefit from new technology. During 1999, Vauxhall became the first car manufacturer in the world to sell its cars on the Internet. Woolworth's, the major high-street department store, recently completed a successful trial of interactive TV, where customers using specially configured digital TV sets accessed the store's 'shopping directory' and ordered goods from the comfort of their own home. What used to be thought of as the 'shopping of the future' is now almost available today.

Travel

Reservation systems, ticketing systems and in-flight services are just a few of the main types of business application used within the travel industry. They all require huge computer systems and databases to store customer and flight information from travel agencies and airline companies situated all over the world. The travel industry has been quick to benefit from the Internet – many airline companies such as British Airways, Lufthansa, American Airlines and British Midland have Web sites, which provide online booking services to their passengers.

Computing in the public sector

The perception of work in the public sector (in schools, hospitals and local government, for instance) has not always been good.

Computing and IT, whilst avoiding many of the problems associated with the public sector (such as the lack of investment, and stifling bureaucracy), has experienced its own challenges, most notably those caused by outsourcing IT departments to other companies.

In the new millennium, there is an air of cautious optimism from IT staff in the public sector. Many of the outsourcing deals have not been as successful as hoped, with the result either of bringing back IT departments in-house or of changing the way the outsourcing is managed to ensure fair play. Much of the old bureaucracy has gone, many working practices have changed and there is a new openness within the sector as a whole.

For the newcomer to computing and IT, the public sector now offers good opportunities for career development up to the highest levels of office. Not only do public sector IT staff tend to stay longer in their jobs than their counterparts in private industry, but they also feel they make a greater social contribution as well. Unfortunately, some ridiculous comparisons are made between IT staff working in the public sector and those working in the private sector, mainly in the areas of pay and promotion. Whilst IT managers cannot always reward staff with huge bonuses in the public sector, many public sector IT staff did receive bonuses for critical millennium work – many being paid well over £2,000.

Contrary to popular belief that the public sector cannot offer a rewarding IT career, the public sector in the UK runs some of the largest and most complex IT projects in Europe. The National Health Service alone is pioneering new technology all the time, allowing the sharing of medical records and clinical data in the quest for greater benefits. Local authorities, which employ over 18,000 IT staff in the UK, use huge IT systems to collect council tax and distribute housing benefit. Whilst these systems are generally not 'leading edge' in the sense that they do not extend our boundaries of knowledge in IT, they are huge, complex and require the skills of many IT professionals to design, build and support.

Throughout the UK and Europe, governments are already developing IT strategies and training programmes to make use of IT in a way that has never happened before. Traditional forms of communication will gradually be replaced with new technologies.

The humble domestic TV set will be used to deliver important forms and information to citizens throughout the country. In fact, it won't be long before a visit to your local post office will reveal a network of Internet-capable PCs rather than a weighing machine and a cash register.

The Post Office

The Post Office is one of the biggest (and earliest) users of information technology in the UK and makes use of a very wide range of computing technologies and methods. It has a central IT unit (with about 1,000 people based in Farnborough, Hants and Chesterfield, Derbyshire), which provides support and services across the Post Office businesses, and there are many more people working on computerized systems within those businesses.

The central unit provides IT career opportunities at three levels:

- A level school-leavers are recruited to posts in the computer operations departments and may carry out jobs such as running batch programs on mainframe computers, or taking and dealing with calls on Post Office IT helpdesks. Once they have more knowledge of computing, many of them move into more specialist jobs.
- Degree students (not necessarily on computing or IT courses) can apply for a limited number of places with the Post Office during or shortly after their last year. Those selected are put through a carefully designed programme of training courses and six-month placements in different departments, with the intention of preparing them to become the senior specialists and managers of the future.
- The other group of IT people joining the Post Office are those who have already gained some knowledge and experience elsewhere. With the size and range of IT activities in the Post Office, there is a steady demand for new people, and promotion can be very fast for the right people. Salary arrangements and other benefits for IT people have to be more flexible than is usual in large organizations to ensure that the Post Office can compete successfully in the very busy and fast-moving IT job market.

Contact information

Contact The Post Office, IT Services, Concept 2000, 250 Farnborough Road, Farnborough, Hants GU14 7LU (tel: 01252 528000).

7 Computing in education

With the focus often placed on business and commerce, it is easy to forget the crucial role IT plays within the academic world. Whether you decide to become a teacher in secondary education or a university researcher, you will be faced with as many challenges as, and in some ways more challenges than, people working in business. With over 400,000 teachers in England and Wales, IT skills are as much in demand within the educational system as they are in the commercial sector.

It is worth remembering that the computer scientists of the future will need to be educated *today* in order for them to fulfil their potential. Thanks to a number of recent initiatives, computing and IT now have a major part to play in education. Information technology is taught as part of the national curriculum from primary school upwards, and is in fact the only fundamentally *new* subject in the national curriculum. In further and higher education, more and more computing-related subjects are being introduced all the time to meet the demands of business and commerce as well as for future research activity.

Opportunities to teach computing and information technology exist in the following institutions:

◆ secondary schools;
◆ city technology colleges (CTCs);
◆ further education (FE) colleges;
◆ sixth form colleges;
◆ universities.

Information technology *is* taught in primary schools, but to teach at this level you first need to learn specialized teaching methods and must be able to teach in a wide range of other subjects as well as information technology.

Working in secondary education

If you want to teach information technology in a state-maintained secondary school you must first become a qualified teacher. This can be achieved in a number of different ways, but they all provide you with, at minimum, qualified teacher status (QTS). In most cases, QTS is achieved by following an approved course of initial teacher training (ITT). Around 30,000 places are available each year for ITT courses, and of those about 14,000 are for secondary education training. Before you start your ITT course, you must have already gained the equivalent of GCSE grade C (or above) in both English language and mathematics. The two main routes to obtain QTS are by completing a degree course or a postgraduate course. These courses are run in schools, colleges and universities throughout the UK.

Degree courses for teacher training

Any one of the following degrees enables you to enter the teaching profession whilst also providing you with a professional qualification. They are all usually four years in length, combining a standard degree with a year of teacher training:

- ◆ BEd (Bachelor of Education – shortened two-year course also available;
- ◆ BA (Bachelor of Arts) with QTS;
- ◆ BSc (Bachelor of Science) with QTS.

The basic minimum requirements for teacher training degrees are five different subjects (grade C or above) at GCSE level or equivalent, including English language and mathematics, plus two

A-levels or equivalent, such as BTEC National Award or GNVQ (General National Vocational Qualification) in computing or IT.

Postgraduate courses for teacher training

For secondary school teaching, the main route is by gaining a PGCE (Postgraduate Certificate in Education) qualification after you have obtained a degree through the normal routes (your degree, however, must contain a strong element of computing or IT). The standard PGCE is a one-year full-time course, which you can either start immediately after gaining your degree or return to after gaining a number of years' work experience. A PGCE for secondary education normally takes one academic year (36 weeks) to complete, including a minimum of 24 weeks' teacher training in a secondary school. There are some PGCE courses that are specific for those wanting to teach information technology at secondary school level; others contain a mixture of IT and other sciences to help reinforce the requirements laid down in the national curriculum.

Where to study for a postgraduate teaching qualification
You can study for a PGCE at the following academic institutions:

- university or college of higher education;
- school or city technology college (school-centred ITT);
- Open University.

Open University PGCE courses
The Open University (OU) now runs distance-learning PGCE courses for secondary courses in IT subjects. These usually take 18 months to complete, combining periods of teaching practice and on-site school projects, making them comparable with a standard PGCE.

Teaching as a second career – mature entry

If you are 24 or over, you have the opportunity to combine 'real' teaching in IT with training that will ultimately lead to gaining a

QTS award. This scheme is known as the Licensed Teacher Scheme (LTS). It was designed mainly for mature entrants into the teaching profession, but is also available to non-graduate teachers who have trained overseas. Becoming a licensed teacher gives you the chance to have some on-the-job training – similar to an apprenticeship. It is particularly useful when there is a shortage of qualified teachers in a certain area.

The main entry requirements for the Licensed Teacher Scheme are that you:

◆ should preferably hold a degree or, if you do not have a degree, you must have two years' successful full-time higher education (or part-time equivalent);
◆ should have demonstrated a standard equivalent to GCSE grade C in English language and mathematics before your licence begins;
◆ must be over 24 years old (unless you are a teacher trained overseas).

Secondary Subject Shortage Scheme

All students on ITT programmes in England covering information technology or on courses covering the 7 to 14 age range in information technology are eligible for financial assistance under the Secondary Subject Shortage Scheme.

Getting started

If you want to teach IT as part of the national curriculum, then it would be a good idea to have some understanding of what the national curriculum is and how IT is taught within it. All schools have copies of the national curriculum and, although it is unlikely that they would let you borrow one, they might let you have a look at it if you made an appointment. Alternatively, you can buy a copy of the national curriculum, either as one complete book, or just the section relating to IT. A cheaper and probably more realistic option, however, is to visit the library.

If you want to start doing a bit of general research into education and current IT teaching issues, it is worth reading the following papers, which also advertise vacancies at all levels of the educational system:

- Monday: *The Times*;
- Tuesday: the *Guardian*;
- Thursday: the *Independent* and the *Daily Telegraph*;
- Friday: the *Times Educational Supplement* or 'TES'.

Teachers' salary

Schoolteachers' pay and conditions are regulated by the Department for Education and Employment. From April 1999, salaries for qualified teachers start at £15,537 for good honours graduates (£17,778 for a teacher starting in inner London). Pay then progresses on a rising scale, depending upon experience and extra responsibilities undertaken.

If you aspire towards a management position, there are many opportunities in teaching. Headteachers and their deputies can earn from £27,258 at a small primary school to over £60,000 at a large secondary school. Alternatively, advanced skills teachers concentrate on classroom work and developing the profession; they are paid from £26,082 to £41,607.

Where can I study for a teaching qualification?

For information on ITT courses (BEd; BSc plus QTS; and BA plus QTS), consult the *UCAS Handbook*. UCAS (Universities and Colleges Admissions Service) handles all applications for university and college courses, and its handbook is essential reading for anyone intending to study at degree level.

Further information

For more information on teaching computing and IT in secondary schools, contact the Teaching Information Line on 01245 454454, or write to The TTA Communication Centre, PO Box 3210, Chelmsford, Essex CM1 3WA (Web site: www.teach-tta.gov.uk).

For more information on undergraduate entry into teaching, and an application form, contact the Universities and Colleges Admissions Service (UCAS) on 01242 222444 or write to UCAS, Rosehill, New Barn Lane, Cheltenham, Gloucestershire GL52 3LZ.

For more information on postgraduate entry into teaching (PGCE courses), and an application form, contact the Graduate Teacher Training Registry on 01242 223707 (if you need more than an information pack, ring 01242 544788) or write to Graduate Teacher Training Registry, Rosehill, New Barn Lane, Cheltenham, Gloucestershire GL52 3LZ.

For more information on the Licensed Teacher Scheme, contact the Licensed Teacher Administration Unit on 01202 897691 or write to Licensed Teacher Administration Unit, Project Place, 1 Princes Road, Ferndown, Dorset BH22 9JG.

For additional information on teacher training in Wales, contact the National Assembly for Wales on 01222 826749, or write to The National Assembly for Wales, FHE3 Division, Cathays Park, Cardiff CF1 3NQ (tel: 01222 825831).

Becoming a teacher in Northern Ireland

The Department of Education for Northern Ireland (DENI) regulates teaching practice and is the prime source of information for careers in teaching. Within the educational system there are different types of schools under the control of 'management committees', which are also the employers of teachers. These committees appoint teachers according to the type of school.

Vacancies for teaching jobs in Northern Ireland can be found from a number of sources, including:

◆ *Belfast Telegraph*;
◆ *Irish News*;
◆ *News Letter*.

Further information

Further information on teaching in Northern Ireland can be obtained by contacting the Department of Education for Northern Ireland on 01247 279279 or by writing to DENI, Rathgael House, Balloo Road, Bangor, County Down BT19 7PR.

Lecturing in a college or university

Teachers who work in further and higher education are normally referred to as lecturers and are paid on a slightly different pay scale to teachers. Whilst you do not normally require a teaching qualification to become a college or university lecturer, you do almost certainly need a degree. A computing degree is preferred, but many other degrees are acceptable if they contain a substantial amount of IT.

There is one main difference between working in a college and a university, and that is the emphasis placed upon research. With public sector funding constantly under threat, universities now need to establish close links with industry in order to obtain funding for new research programmes and new staff. As a result, many universities are more interested in what research opportunities potential lecturers can bring to the university (and therefore what private funding they might attract), as opposed to their specific teaching skills. Competition is fierce for these positions; if you *do* want to become a university lecturer, you ideally require:

◆ a good honours degree in an IT subject (preferably a 2:1 or 1st class);
◆ a higher degree (MSc, MPhil, PhD, etc);
◆ specific research interests that match the university's own research programme.

Getting started
Most, if not all, of the lectureships available in UK colleges and universities (and sometimes in foreign universities too) are advertised in the *Times Educational Supplement*.

Salary
Salaries for lecturers in colleges and universities can vary enormously, depending on the institution, funding levels and local demand. Starting salaries for a graduate can be as low as £13,000 but, if you already possess industrial or research experience or have a higher degree, salaries tend to be higher – around the £18,000 mark.

Working in a university computer department

This vacancy for a computer assistant, advertised during December 1999, explains the career opportunities within a university computer services department extremely well:

Job Title: Computer Assistant
Salary: £11,200–£13,456

Role and responsibilities:
Working on the site's Help Desk, you will be the first point of contact for the computing support provided by the University Computer Services Department. As this work involves a high degree of contact with students, you should have a pleasant and welcoming manner. Main duties include:

◆ Help in resolution of users' problems.
◆ Provide advice to users and identify specialist support needs as required.
◆ To assist in the preparation of documentation, enabling users to use installed software packages.
◆ To assist with the installation and configuration of local computer and network equipment.
◆ To assist with the investigation and correction of reported hardware and software faults and liaise with suppliers and departmental staff where necessary.

Personal skills required:
You should be able to communicate well – you will need to explain technical subjects clearly and frequently to inexperienced computer users. Experience in an advisory/help desk role would be advantageous.

Technical skills required:
A basic understanding of IT and Windows 95/NT is essential, as is experience of word-processing, spreadsheet and database software (especially Microsoft product offerings). However, the ability to acquire new technical skills is also as important as those you already possess.

Qualifications:
Normally 4 GCSEs at Ordinary level or equivalent plus appropriate keyboard skills and practical experience of computing equipment and software.

Funded research

Do not be misled into thinking the only way to achieve success in the IT profession is through the high-profile world of commercial computing, where salaries and benefit packages can seem irresistible.

Research is an exciting place for the IT professional, providing many opportunities to use and develop computer systems, often using state-of-the-art systems that would rarely be seen in the commercial sector. With investment returning to the IT world after some bleak periods, the opportunities for research have never been greater. Research projects currently attracting funding include:

◆ computer vision systems;
◆ computer modelling and simulation;
◆ virtual-reality systems;
◆ cybernetics.

Generally, there are two main routes into research: studying for a postgraduate degree by research; and applying for a salaried research post, usually in a university.

Postgraduate degrees by research

Degrees by research are different from 'standard' postgraduate degrees, as they tend to be awarded purely on the result of a research project and the submission of a written thesis or dissertation. The main degrees that are offered for research purposes are MPhil, DPhil and PhD, although some institutions do offer an MSc by research. If you intend applying for one of these degrees, you will almost certainly need a very good first degree in computing or a closely related discipline. Students undertaking postgraduate research are eligible for funding (known as a bursary), which is usually in the region of £5,000.

Salaried research

If you want to join a university research project (usually funded by one of the European agencies), you should apply for a post as a research assistant, which carries a salary (vacancies will be advertised in the *Times Educational Supplement*). This post will normally be for a fixed-length term and you will need a very good computing degree, and possibly even a higher degree as well (such as an MSc or PhD). Although research assistants often work unsupervised, they will usually report to a research director during the project, especially if it is funded externally. Typical salaries for a research assistant are between £14,000 and £20,000.

Case Study

Richard *is a computer studies lecturer.*

'After joining the IT industry as a computing graduate, I soon realized that I was not using and developing my interpersonal skills as much as I would have liked. I've always enjoyed talking about IT issues as much as I have enjoyed the technical side of things, so it was only a matter of time before I started to look for a job in the teaching profession (although I knew very little about it at the time). If I had one worry, it was that I might end up becoming something out of "Grange Hill" – losing all my computing skills but being a dab hand with the blackboard!

'Finding a suitable job was relatively easy; vacancies for college lecturers appear in the *Times Educational Supplement* every week. I think my experience of industry helped me a lot in my interview (which included the principal of the college and various heads of department), as the college was keen to keep up to date with the "real world" of IT. Coming straight from industry, the college sent me on a City and Guilds course to learn the basics of teaching in further education before I started my first term, which was really helpful.

'I have a wide and varied programme of courses to teach, ranging from short one-day courses on computer programming to HND level systems analysis and design. Funding is a problem at the moment though, and so I have to teach an evening class at the moment, just until the college can afford a part-time lecturer to ease my workload.

'Of course, I also have non-teaching responsibilities; I provide a "pastoral" role for my students, and I do make time for them should they wish to discuss their problems with me, whatever they are – a responsibility which I take very seriously.'

8 Occupations within computing and IT departments

Most organizations have an IT department, which manages all the organization's IT activities. There are slight differences in the overall structure of IT departments, but most have a similar structure to that shown in Figure 8.1. Typically, IT departments are structured around the various functions the department must perform as a whole, such as development and support. It is worth spending some time at this stage considering what area of work appeals to you; support or development is an obvious choice, but then again, you may want to go straight into a sales or marketing role.

Within this chapter, I try to provide as much relevant information as possible for each of the areas discussed, but remember, all companies have a slightly different approach to IT, so this information can only be general in nature. The individual case studies in this chapter are, however, specific to individuals who have first-hand experience of working within the IT industry. Treat these as 'insider knowledge' from people who have been successful in their own career development. If you need a source of inspiration to get your IT career started, consider these case studies as your guiding light.

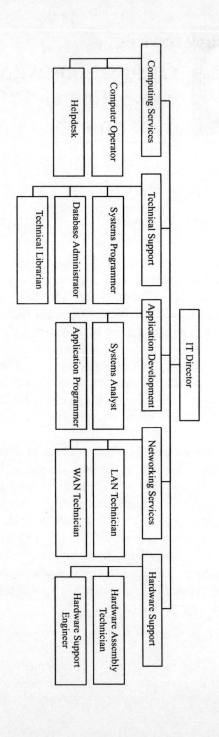

Figure 8.1 The structure of a typical commerical IT department

Computing services

The computing services team structure is shown in Figure 8.2.

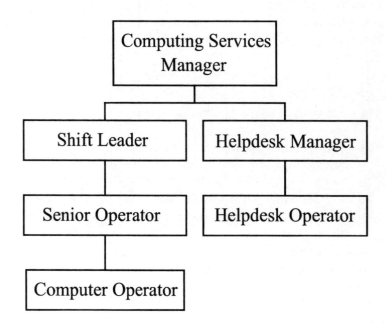

Figure 8.2   The computing services team structure

The computer operator

Over the last few years, the role of the computer operator has changed significantly, becoming an important function within the IT department. Computer operators usually provide direct (first-line) support for the computer system, often 24 hours a day, every day of the year (they are often referred to as '24×7' support). Not only do operators keep the system working within agreed limits of availability (9 am to 5 pm, for instance), but they are also expected to investigate any problems on the computer system and take the appropriate action to fix it. If they cannot fix the problem, they pass it on to the next line of support (second-line support), which means calling one of the support teams, such as the systems programmers or network technicians.

Traditionally, computer operators only worked with mainframe computers but, with the increase in client-server systems, today's computer operators may well have to manage many different computer platforms and operating systems (such as MVS, Unix and NT) and have a basic knowledge of local and wide area networking.

Main tasks
The main tasks of the computer operator are:

◆ taking system backups on to computer tape;
◆ scheduling daily, weekly and monthly work on the computer, eg monthly payroll applications;
◆ loading computer tapes into tape drives for processing;
◆ ensuring user applications have been started and stopped at the correct times;
◆ producing statistics on the performance of the computer;
◆ identifying and resolving computer system errors;
◆ providing general support for the computer system and the applications running on it.

Many computer operators must work shifts to ensure the computer system is available every day of the year. Whilst this may not suit everyone, many operators enjoy shift work, liking especially the bonus shift payments on top of their normal salary (often in the region of 33 per cent).

Salary
Trainee computer operators earn £11,000 upwards. Computer operators earn £13,000–£25,000.

Case Study

John *is a shift leader.*

'When I left school at 16, I wasn't really sure what I wanted to do, although I knew I had more than an interest in computing. On the qualifications front, I did have maths and computing O levels, so I applied for a job in the operations department of a local manufacturer. When I arrived for my first day of work, I was pleasantly surprised to find that no one in the operations team had a degree, as I'd thought it would be essential for this sort of job

'I soon realized why: the type of work we did was specific to our computer – an IBM mainframe – and a degree would not have provided the required skills. After a few months and a fair amount of on-the-job training, I was soon performing all the duties expected of an operator, such as rerunning batch jobs which had failed and diagnosing networking problems (we have a high-speed fibre-optic link between ourselves and one of our major suppliers).

'After two enjoyable years as a computer operator, I moved jobs and I am now a shift leader with one of the privatized water companies – which means I now have responsibility for other operators as well as the computers!'

The helpdesk operator

The helpdesk is the area within the IT department that provides general help and advice to all the users of the computer system. Working with users who are experiencing problems with their IT hardware or software, the helpdesk operator provides the first (and most important) point of contact between the IT department and the business departments within the organization.

Skills required
Skills required for a helpdesk operator are:

◆ patience and understanding (not everyone is computer-literate!);

♦ a pleasing manner (by the time many users have contacted the helpdesk, they will have gone mad trying to get their system to work and they will probably take it out on you!);
♦ a general understanding of how computer systems work (many users are confident in talking about how their PC is configured and how their applications work – are you?).

Whilst some helpdesk operators are highly skilled computer technicians, often resolving lengthy and complex user problems, the average helpdesk operator performs the following tasks:

♦ records user problems;
♦ resolves day-to-day problems (such as users forgetting their system passwords);
♦ informs users of any maintenance work taking place on the computer system (which might prevent them from using it);
♦ passes more complex problems to the support teams for fixing;
♦ contacts computer manufacturers and suppliers if an error is identified with one of their products.

Salary
Helpdesk operators earn £10,000–£15,000. Technical helpdesk operators earn £13,000–£20,000.

Application development

The application development team structure is shown in Figure 8.3.

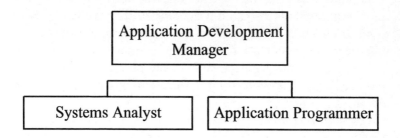

Figure 8.3   The application development team structure

The systems analyst

The role of the systems analyst (or just 'analyst') is one of the most challenging within the IT industry, as it is the systems analyst who must initially convert a business requirement (such as 'we need a better order-processing system') into a series of IT requirements that computer programmers and database designers will understand. Analysts often work with other IT professionals and business users as members of a project until the IT solution has been built and implemented – the systems development project.

Historically, once analysts had produced the IT requirements, their role was to a large extent finished. Nowadays, many analysts also write the application code after capturing the business requirements – in essence performing an analyst/programmer role. Analyst programmers are becoming more and more popular as many IT companies now require staff with a mixture of programming and analytical skills.

Once an IT project has started, usually with the publication of a proposal document, the systems analyst must begin to understand the customer's current system (regardless of whether it is implemented on a computer or not). Only by identifying the business processes and functions in the existing system can the analyst be confident that the new system will be developed correctly.

It is important that the systems analyst focuses closely on the users' requirements throughout the project and what they expect to be delivered at the end of it – any misunderstandings by the user or the analyst could seriously affect the success of the project. To help prevent this happening, the analyst refers to a document produced at the start of the project, the 'terms of reference', which identifies the objectives and scope of the project, and clarifies exactly what is expected by the customer.

Skills required

The role of a systems analyst is often a complex one, combining many different technical and managerial skills. As much of the work involves gathering and collating information from the business, as well as producing technical requirements, you will find that most systems analysts possess the following:

- a clear and logical approach to problem-solving (can you ask the right questions?);
- good verbal communication (can you express your thoughts clearly?);
- 'customer-facing' skills (business jargon for being well presented and professional when dealing with customers);
- the ability to draw business processes and data flows clearly;
- business skills (can you appreciate the customer's problem from a business perspective, and are you able to identify important business risks as well as potential benefits?).

After looking at this demanding list of skills, you can understand why many systems analysts have degrees or a fair amount of business experience. Systems analysis is not an easy role into IT for the inexperienced starter – even for an IT graduate.

Salary

A graduate systems analyst can expect to earn anything between £15,000 and £20,000 a year. With experience, systems analysts (or business consultants as many are now called) can easily attract salaries in the region of £30,000–£50,000 a year.

Case Study

Clare *is a business systems analyst.*

'In 1987, I graduated from university with a degree in business studies, with the intention of being in management by the time I was 30. I'm pleased to say that didn't happen as I'm now thoroughly enjoying my current career as a business systems analyst with a major manufacturing company, based in London. I joined the company's graduate recruitment scheme as a graduate trainee, and became a trainee analyst by the time the programme had completed. For the next two years I assisted in several small analysis projects, working in a small team. Although I found it interesting, I also found it difficult at first, especially when it came to modelling business systems with diagrams such as entity-relationship diagrams and dataflow diagrams. I think my business degree did help me in the early stages, as understanding the business and the user requirements is vital for this sort of work. Gaining promotion to an analyst, for the next four years I performed the role of lead analyst in a support environment. During that time I was responsible for documenting user requirements and producing and updating system specifications, which I passed to the programming team to code. I am now a systems analyst, which means I am responsible for the whole process of requirements analysis, producing functional and system specifications and terms of reference within my section. I now have to justify my decisions to the IT manager, so I have just been sent on a cost–benefit analysis course to help me. It's a demanding job; a mistake so early on in a project could put the "cat amongst the pigeons"! In my current position, I get the chance to meet lots of people and perform my objectives with very little supervision, which is what I like. In many ways, I am responsible for many of my actions, but having been in an analysis role since joining the company, I've got a good idea how things are done!'

The application programmer

Application development is the largest occupational area within IT for a very good reason – it is through application software that IT delivers most benefit to the business. Application programmers historically wrote programs in languages such as COBOL on mainframe computers, but today a lot of applications are written using PC-based software packages such as Visual Basic and Java.

Main tasks

Regardless of the programming language used, an application programmer needs to be able to:

◆ Design the computer program using a series of 'English-like' statements that document the logical way of solving the problem, for example:

```
for each customer in customer database
        read customer's account details
        if customer's balance < 0
        then
                send warning letter to customer
                set account status to 'overdrawn'
        endif
endfor
```

◆ Write (or modify existing) application code.
◆ Test the program to ensure there are no errors ('bugs') within it.
◆ Document the computer program so it can be maintained and modified at a later date. It is often the case that the person who maintains a computer program is not the person who wrote it – many programs are passed over to application support teams when they have been written, freeing up the original programmer to work on a different project.

Skills required

The skills required are:

◆ logical thought (try completing the popular 'logic puzzle' magazines!);

♦ the ability to produce clear, understandable and well-struc-
tured program code (someone else may have to maintain
your program later);

♦ the ability to produce solutions that match customer
requirements (you might think it is a great piece of code,
but does it do the job?).

Most application programmers work in a team managed by a
senior programmer. Within the team there are probably a number
of experienced application programmers and a small number of
junior programmers. Whilst they all write program code, it is
likely that the experienced programmers will design and write the
main parts of the application, leaving the junior programmers to
write and test the smaller and less crucial parts of the application.

Salary
Junior programmers earn £12,000 upwards. Computing graduates earn £16,000–£20,000.

Case Study

Diane *is a mainframe application programmer.*

'Originally, the idea of entering the computer profession was not one of my
career aims, which is why I decided to study for a degree in English language. On graduating, I realized that I did not really want to become an
English teacher, so, realizing that IT was going to be with us for some time, I
decided to study for an MSc conversion course in information technology.
The course allowed graduates in one discipline to grasp the basics of
another subject within a year – it was an intensive course, but well worth
the many hours I spent in the computer labs. I found this course really
interesting, and I even managed to use some of my English skills when we
studied artificial intelligence and natural language processing (getting computers to understand speech). Feeling more confident with IT, I joined
Rolls-Royce, as I wanted to work for a large company that had a graduate
training programme. Within six months of joining I had learnt the basics of
programming in PL/1, which is a 'high-level' language used for business
computing. I soon realized the importance of writing 'structured' programs,
as it not only makes them easier to design and write, but also much easier
for other people to maintain as well. After 'graduating' from the computer

training centre, I started to use my new skills in a small project team based in the computer building. At first, I was just writing the odd line here and there – basically amending other people's programs to perform slightly better, but not long after, I was writing complex programs myself. At times, I find it hard to believe how far I've progressed in the IT world, when I could so easily have joined the teaching profession!'

Technical support

The technical support team structure is shown in Figure 8.4.

The systems programmer

Within all computer systems, there are a number of programs and utilities that are used by the computer system itself; collectively they are called 'systems software'. Writing, installing or maintaining this software is the main task performed by the systems programmer.

Systems programmers often have to manipulate special files or execute complex commands as part of their work. As these affect the computer system, and there is always a risk of something going wrong, causing a major problem, these tasks are sometimes performed at weekends when the computer system is not required by the users.

Main tasks
The main tasks of the systems programmer are:

- installing new versions of computer software (applications and operating systems);
- fixing system-level errors on the computer;
- configuring systems software, eg data backup utilities;
- tuning the computer system;
- controlling access to and security of the computer system;
- providing second-line support when required.

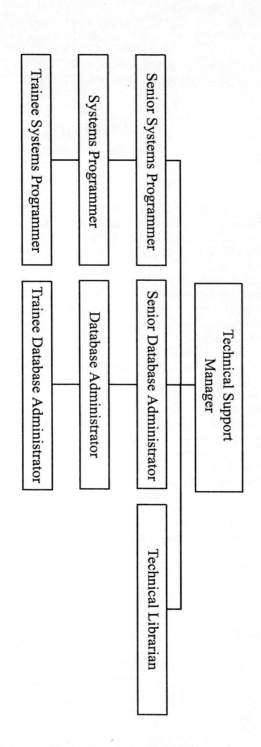

Figure 8.4 The technical support team structure

Salary

Trainee systems programmers earn £13,000–£15,000. Graduate systems programmers earn £16,000–£20,000.

Case Study

Chris is a mainframe systems programmer.

'I did a three-year BSc chemistry course at Surrey University. I obtained a summer job with an ICI research station where I found that a PhD was the minimum requirement to make any reasonable progress in the chemical industry. I therefore decided to get a job in the computer industry, another interest of mine.

'I joined Datasolve as graduate trainee in the operations department. This gave me a good grounding in how a commercial computer system is put together. I progressed to running a shift of 12 staff running multiple machines across multiple sites and performed a wide range of tasks in many different areas, including console operations, data communications, tape handling, printing and disaster recovery.

'I moved out of operations into mainframe automation first with Datasolve and later with the Post Office. My operations experience was essential, enabling me to program the computer systems to perform the required actions. Automation mainly consists of determining the most appropriate actions (rather than those currently being carried out) and then configuring the system software to perform them. Recently I have become involved in a large project to automate and integrate all the other computer platforms used within the business.

'I have found my scientific training useful for analysing operational requirements and writing various reports in a clear, objective manner. My operations experience has proved invaluable, and has given me an in-depth understanding of how the various components of a complex computer environment fit together.'

The database administrator

Many business applications access large amounts of information, which is stored in a database. Whilst there are many different types of database available today, 'relational' databases, such as Microsoft

Access and Oracle, are probably the most popular. When information held in the database is added, updated or deleted by a user, it is called a 'transaction'. As you can imagine, over time, as more users run transactions against the database, it gradually increases in size and, if left unmanaged, will eventually cause problems. It is vitally important that the structure of the database and the complex relationships between the data are maintained regularly by the database administrator, otherwise inconsistencies may arise.

Main tasks

The main tasks of the database administrator are:

◆ maintaining the integrity of the data within the database (is the data valid and accurate?);
◆ ensuring the database can be recovered in the event of an error (eg computer crash, virus or power failure);
◆ tuning the database (will the database still perform well when more data is added to it?);
◆ sizing the database (how large will it need to be in the future?).

Salary

Trainee database administrators earn £13,000–£16,000. Graduate database administrators earn £18,000–£20,000.

Case Study

John is a database administrator.

'When I was at school all those years ago, I was not very academic and, leaving school with very few qualifications, ended up working in the mail room of our local sweet factory. I can remember it well; it was very boring and routine. This all changed when the company had a mainframe computer installed some years later. Wanting a change from sorting mail and parcels, I applied for a position as a trainee computer operator in the computer room. I got it, but I didn't get away from sorting paper, as my first task was to keep the huge printers stocked up with paper all day! Eventually, I became a computer operator, and after a few more years' experience and attending a few technical courses, I became an MVS systems programmer. Having been in the company all my working life, my role became quite easy to be honest, as I understood all the user applications and how they ran on the mainframe computer. However, the company was growing faster than the computer system, so the company decided to install IBM's relational database management system (DB2), to store all the company stock and price information. This was about the biggest project the company had ever tackled since the installation of the mainframe computer and whilst it was exciting to be part of an IBM project, I was a bit nervous, as I had been asked to install the database system software on the mainframe! The company sent me on an IBM course in London to install and configure DB2, which lasted a week, by which time I was confident in what I had to do back at work. The project went very well, and I was promoted to database administrator within the computer department – the first one ever. To be honest, things were hectic at first and I ended up working quite a few weekends to tune the database parameters as it was the only time I could get to close the database down without affecting the users. I'm glad to say the system is working fine now, requiring very little maintenance, which has allowed me time to get involved with the next database project, which involves working with UNIX – something I've never used before!'

The technical librarian

Unfortunately, the IT dream of being able to work in a paperless office by the 21st century has not yet materialized! Even now, with many computer manuals being distributed on CD, the storage and management of this information is still crucially important – it could mean the difference between a computer system being fixed in five minutes or five hours.

Main tasks

A technical librarian is usually responsible for managing all the information within the technical library, regardless of whether this information is in the form of books, manuals, training videos, CDs or Internet-based material. The technical librarian provides an important service to business users and IT staff by supplying information they need from the library, such as books for training purposes or technical manuals to help resolve a problem.

Salary
Technical librarians earn £12,000–£20,000 (depending on the size and nature of the information managed).

Case Study

Mark *is a technical librarian working for a UK airline company.*

'I joined the company as an office junior and it was here I gained my first experience of IT – as a user. A few years later, I was sent on a course and obtained a postgraduate diploma in information and library management. Feeling confident in managing information, I joined the IT department as an IT librarian in 1996.

'Whilst most people think that working in a library is just about shuffling books, technical libraries are different. Not only do I have to manage computer manuals, I also have to maintain information held on CD ROM and diskette. Keeping track of information within the IT department is extremely important, especially things like version numbers of software and financial information such as maintenance agreements.

'Since then, I've been getting involved in developing different types of information systems using multi-media, such as the Web. I've already helped set up a pilot project to develop a company intranet so that corporate information (and details of how to book cheap holidays!) can be made available to everyone in the company who has access to a PC.

'I've gained lots of HTML skills, originally by downloading a tutorial I found on the Web. Since then, I've started using Microsoft Front Page to help me design a Web site, which is ideal for me, as I've had no formal training in this area at all. Luckily, it's such an interesting area, I've taught myself many new skills – I'm even confident using Java in my Web pages now, something I never thought I would learn as a librarian!'

Networking services

The networking team structure is shown in Figure 8.5.

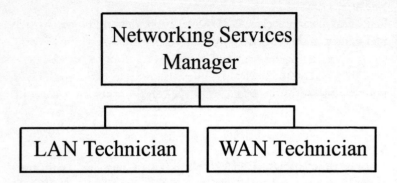

Figure 8.5   The networking team structure

The LAN technician

Many departments now need to share business information with other users within the same organization; they can do this by using one or more local area networks (LANs), which connect many users together.

Many PCs and UNIX systems are now connected to a LAN within the organization. The LAN technician must be able to design reliable networks so that data and applications can be shared by everyone who needs them. This is not as simple as it first seems, especially if there are many different types of computer within the organization.

Main tasks
The main tasks of the LAN technician are:

◆ connecting computers to LANs, on mainframe, mid-range or desktop platforms;
◆ designing and building networks using technologies such as Ethernet and token ring;
◆ configuring network software to add new connections or restrict access to certain users on the network;
◆ identifying and resolving errors on the network (such as data congestion and slow response).

Skills required

LAN technicians need knowledge of LAN software and communication protocols, such as TCP/IP (transmission control protocol/Internet protocol – a networking protocol popular in UNIX networks and on the Internet). They also need knowledge of LAN networking hardware, such as network cards, token ring adaptors and hubs.

Salary

LAN technicians earn £12,000–£15,000. Graduates with networking experience earn £18,000–£20,000.

Case Study

Mike is a network technician responsible for a number of departmental LANs.

'Having spent five years working for a large retail chain as a programmer, I was never really interested in networking at first. Like most of my colleagues, I did not really appreciate networking, and I suppose I just saw it as messing around with lots of cables and switches. My opinion soon changed when the company expanded its mainframe computer system to incorporate UNIX and PC systems. All of a sudden, the network became something we could all associate with, as we all started having Ethernet cards slotted in our PCs and we were all given IP addresses showing our unique address on the network. I realized that working in the network team could be an exciting move for me, and I haven't looked back since. The company sent me on a few basic courses to learn about the major protocols used on the network – TCP/IP and SNMP – and within a few weeks the whole fuzzy area of networking became clear! The networking team are now looking into development of the Internet, fire-walls (a UNIX server which protects the rest of the network against unauthorized access) and lots of other exciting new developments that are happening within the IT and networking world. As the IT department is constantly expanding its PC LAN, I'm hoping I can learn more about NT, and maybe gain certification in the future – quite an achievement for an ex-COBOL programmer!'

The WAN technician

The term 'wide area network' (WAN) applies to any type of computer network that covers a large physical area. Typically WANs are used to transfer information between companies in different geographical locations, either within the same country or worldwide. These sorts of communications system are extremely complex, requiring not only an understanding of networking equipment such as bridges, routers and network controllers, but also of the telecommunications systems used to relay the data, such as high-speed digital telephone lines or satellite communications. The WAN technician often works closely with telecommunications companies and networking hardware suppliers in order to build data networks using public or private telephone lines across the country. Sometimes the backbone network is already in place, which means extra users can be added on to it by the addition of a piece of networking hardware; sometimes that whole 'branch' of the network needs to be added. Once the WAN has been installed, a lot of time is spent monitoring and tuning the network, which could be routing data between many towns and cities, even countries, all the time. As you can imagine with such a widespread system containing many connections, the scope for error is quite high. Not only that, but the WAN technician must identify faults on the network that might have been caused by a failing network component hundreds of miles away!

Main tasks
The main tasks of the WAN technician are:

◆ to install (or commission a network or telecommunications supplier to install) network hardware and attach it to the telecommunications links;
◆ to install software to monitor and configure the network (such as reporting errors in connection or high usage, which may cause response time problems);
◆ to document the company's network structure in order to help manage and expand the network (maybe using PC-based network modelling tools);

◆ to build any test networks that might be needed by the organization.

Skills required
WAN technicians need a knowledge of WAN technologies and protocols – such as X25, TCP/IP, frame relay and ATM (asynchronous transfer method) – and a good understanding of the services and products offered by telecommunications companies.

Salary
WAN technicians earn £12,000–£15,000. Graduates with networking experience earn £16,000–£20,000.

Hardware support

The hardware support team structure is shown in Figure 8.6.

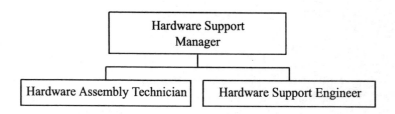

Figure 8.6   The hardware support team structure

The hardware assembly technician

Many new computer systems are custom-built to user requirements, and it is the job of the hardware assembly technician to assemble and test such systems. This type of work typically involves building computers, such as PCs, by 'plugging' together a number of required components such as disk drives, power supplies, circuit boards and cooling systems. Obviously, for this sort of role an interest in electronics is useful, as well as a general understanding of computers. Generally, a degree is not required for this role, as many companies take on school-leavers with GCSEs and provide training.

Salary
Hardware assembly technicians and hardware test engineers earn £10,000–£15,000.

The hardware support engineer

Computer equipment, just like any other electronic equipment, is bound to fail sometime during its life span. Whilst the average household can survive a day or two without the TV or washing machine, the average company starts to lose money if vital computer equipment is not fixed as soon as possible. The hardware support engineer plays an important role in ensuring the computer hardware is working correctly by providing such services as:

- ◆ replacing or repairing faulty computer equipment;
- ◆ performing diagnostics on devices suspected of being faulty (usually by running diagnostic computer software, which identifies faults and recommends solutions);
- ◆ installing and testing new computer hardware.

All of the major computer suppliers have their own hardware engineers who provide service and support for customers in their local area, so a fair amount of travel can be involved in shipping parts to customers and installing them at their computer site. Whilst a good understanding of computer hardware design, such as reduced instruction set computer (RISC) technologies, is expected for this role, a degree is not necessary as vendor-specific skills are often preferred to 'general' hardware skills.

Salary
Hardware support engineers earn £15,000–£20,000.

Freelance IT contractors

All of the major reports on employment opportunities commissioned predict there will be a huge rise in the number of contract IT vacancies, especially now businesses are planning many post-2000 IT projects. Whilst this is no great surprise, it does reflect the changing values of both employees and employers within the IT industry. Flexibility is the key to working as a freelance contractor; if you are willing to work anywhere, on any project, you can expect to be rewarded well for your efforts.

Most contractors work for themselves in the sense that they own their own company, into which their salary is paid by the company they are working for. Whilst the idea of being the managing director of your own company may boost your ego, it does have its drawbacks. For one thing, you will have to pay National Insurance premiums both as an employee *and* as an employer. You will also have to pay for any training you require (unless you can make 'an arrangement' with your employer) and lose your entitlement to company sick pay.

Contractors are required in all the major areas of IT support and development for all sorts of reasons, the main one being to source a short-term skills requirement on a major project. For this reason, most contracts are between 3 and 6 months' duration, but contracts of 12 months are now becoming more common. Hundreds of jobs for contractors are advertised every week in *Computing* and *Computer Weekly*, but there are a number of IT magazines specifically aimed at those working as contractors, such as *Freelance Informer* and *Computer Contractor*.

Further information
Computing/Computer Contractor
VNU Business Publications
The Circulation Manager
VNU House
32–34 Broadwick Street
London W1A 2HG
Tel: (0171) 316 9000

Computer Weekly/Freelance Informer
Reed Business Publishing
Circulation Manager
Quadrant House
The Quadrant
Sutton
Surrey SM2 5AS
Tel: (01444) 441212

Freelance Informer helpline: (01622) 778222

Salary
On average, a freelance IT contractor can expect to earn £1,000 a week. Well-paid contracts for skills in demand can attract salaries of £2,000 a week.

Case Study

Dave *is a freelance computer contractor.*

'As far as qualifications go with regard to computers when I left school, I had none. Although I did do O level computer studies and was top of the class, everybody failed the exam, including myself.

'Armed with only 3 O levels in maths, physics and biology, my career aim of computers was way off target. However, I was lucky and I managed to get on the YTS (Youth Training Scheme) to become an office trainee.

'I was at the YTS for just under four months before I was offered a job as computer operator at the local council offices, so at 18 my computer career began. I had hit my target, even though I had to do shift work. I stayed with the council for about two years, gaining experience with mainframe computers.

'My career really took off with my next job – again with mainframes, but with a more technical involvement. Excelling at programming and job correction, I was promoted through the ranks of operator, senior operator and then shift leader quite quickly. Here I began to teach myself the COBOL programming language – if you want to get somewhere you have to motivate yourself; no one is going to give it to you.

'I left the company after two and a half years, only months before it folded, and moved into the realms of technical support with a different company – no more shift work like before and my programming skills came in handy. However, it was a larger company and the technical involvement was limited.

'Accepting my next job after two and a half years was another career turn – a smaller company, but the technical exposure was enormous. Here, I was exposed to UNIX and I wanted to get involved, but was initially rejected, so I put myself on a weekend UNIX training course and a City and Guilds C programming language course in the evenings – which I passed. I think I proved something to the company, and with that I became involved with UNIX.

'After two years with the company I was made redundant, but was asked to stay around during the handover period whilst the FM company got to grips with the company's computer systems.

'Being unemployed was not fun. However, it gave me the chance to revise my skills and to look into something that I had been thinking about for some time – contracting. Maybe being made redundant had been a blessing in disguise. After two months' redundancy, I had my first contract with my own company in the UNIX market. My career now has rocket boosters attached. I can now obtain more training by putting myself on more courses and gain more skills to make myself more marketable.

'I haven't looked back since.'

9 Occupations outside the IT department

The aim of this chapter is to give you a brief understanding of some of the jobs and roles that are not usually performed within a commercial IT department. They are still IT-related jobs, of course, but they are not concerned with developing or supporting commercial business systems. Again, as in the previous chapter, the case studies included in this chapter have been written by IT professionals who actually perform the roles highlighted. You can treat what they say as first-hand, accurate accounts of how they entered the IT industry and how their careers have developed within it.

Computer game development

The structure of a typical computer game development studio is shown in Figure 9.1.

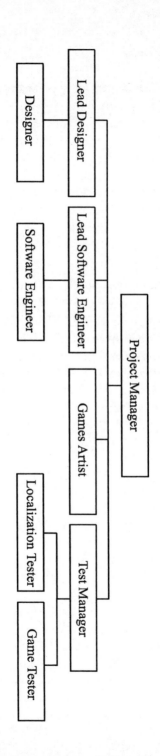

Figure 9.1 The structure of a typical computer game development studio

Software engineer

Owing to the complex way in which games are developed, games programmers are often referred to as 'software engineers', although this is not standard throughout the industry. Software engineers working for games companies develop games software from an initial idea or design. There is often more than one programmer working in a team, and each programmer works on a separate piece of the game. Whilst games programmers today have the benefit of being able to use sophisticated computer packages, programming skills are still extremely important.

Skills required

Despite what you might think, this is not a job for amateur programmers who like playing computer games. Modern games programming has a high mathematical emphasis and requires a disciplined approach to programming. Even if you have taught yourself how to write computer programs from a tutorial program, it does not mean you possess the right professional skills to work as a programmer, such as team-working and problem-solving. For this reason, most companies expect you to possess a good degree (2:1 or 1st class) from a respected university. The degree should be in one of the following subjects: computing, software engineering, mathematics, physics or engineering.

Whilst there are always junior positions available, where a degree is not always necessary, do not hold out too much hope if you only have GCSEs or A levels. If you do not have a degree, you must be able to demonstrate that you are an *exceptionally* good programmer who can write structured and easily maintainable code. Most games companies will want to review a sample game or routine you have written to prove your programming competence.

A good working knowledge of programming languages used for gaming, such as C, C++ and Assembler, is needed if you want to be a games programmer. In addition, a knowledge of artificial intelligence (AI) techniques and 3-D programming techniques is useful.

Games artist

A computer games artist is responsible for creating the images used within a computer game, such as characters, scenery and on-screen instructions. If the game uses complex moving images, specialist graphics packages such as 3D Studio MAX are used, which save a lot of time and effort (and consequently cost).

Skills required
As you might expect, to be a games artist you need to be a good artist rather than an IT expert. Games software companies can teach artists relevant computer skills, but they can't teach an IT expert how to be a good artist!

Games designer

A games designer performs a number of roles, depending on the size of the development studio. If the studio employs just a few people, the games designer may well be involved in everything from designing the game (plot, characters and scenery), and writing manuals and in-game text to planning how the special visual effects and music editing tasks need to be incorporated into the game. The designer often works closely with the project manager from the initial concept to the finished computer game.

Skills required
A games designer performs a crucial role in the development of a computer game, and it is not an area you would move into without previous experience of the games industry. In practice, a games designer needs a number of skills, such as games design, project management, scheduling and research. To help in this role, many designers use specialist computer packages written by the development studio (as opposed to buying an 'off-the-shelf' package).

Games tester

The games tester plays an important (and enviable) role in the development of a computer game. Testing must be methodical and thorough to ensure the game has been written to the design specification, incorporating any short cuts, tricks and bonus screens that may have been included in the game. Whilst casual playing of the game may detect the obvious errors, only many hours of testing every option and route within the game will uncover the smaller errors, which if not picked up before distribution will cause many problems.

Skills required
PC and game-playing skills are essential, but good planning skills and a methodical approach to work are equally important. To be able to test a game, the tester must first understand how the game *should* work, considering for instance what the screens should look like, how the controls should operate and how well the music is synchronized to events within the game. The ability to grasp and manage complex interdependent tasks quickly is vital in this role.

Localization tester

Before games written for the UK market can be sold in other countries, they may require changes to be made to the screen displays or the instruction manuals. It is the role of the localization tester to test such games during their transition from the original English into the localized version that will be used in the country of purchase. The localization tester will ensure all translations made are correct and proof-read all the manuals.

Skills required
Fluency in foreign languages (mainly European) is essential, as is a good understanding of the English language. A good understanding of PCs is important – and you must enjoy playing computer games!

What will the work be like?

A career in the computer games industry involves working in a highly competitive market with many commercial pressures (just think of Christmas games sales every year). With so many excellent games companies operating within the sector, often the only difference between success and failure is how quickly they can get their game into the shops.

More often than not, you work in a team throughout the life cycle of the product, from designing the game to completing the finished version ready for sale. During the early stages of development, the average team size is small (around six people), but towards the end of the project, when pressure to get the game completed and marketed is greater, the team will reach nearer 30 in number. Throughout the project you need to communicate with non-IT people, such as artists and sound engineers, so communication and planning skills are important. These skills are taught on degree courses, which is another reason why there is a demand for high-calibre graduates in this industry.

Salary

The average entry-level salary is around £17,000–£19,000 for all positions, rising to over £40,000. In addition, you can expect to earn royalties based on sales.

Further information

A useful source of information for anyone interested in this area is any one of the many magazines specializing in computer games. *The Edge* is a particularly good source of information, providing details on the products, companies and career opportunities within the industry, and is read by many existing games designers and programmers.

Specific information on particular game companies and development studios can usually be found on their own Web sites (again, have a look in *The Edge* for company information).

Case Study

Chris *is a junior games programmer.*

'I left school at 16 with O levels and no definite career plans, although I was quite interested in computers. As luck would have it, I saw an advert for a government-sponsored IT training scheme and joined the same day.

'As part of the training scheme, I started work in a local computer shop selling microcomputers and computer peripherals. Although I enjoyed meeting people and talking about computers, software and accessories, I preferred working in the offices, where I was allowed to help fix some of the computers. Luckily, as I showed an interest in the more fundamental aspects of computers, I was allowed to help write some of their own games software. At this stage, it was nothing too complicated, mainly just understanding how the game was written and the routines used to load the software on to the microcomputer. I was still keen, so they taught me Assembler language, which is what most of the games programs and utilities were written in.

'A few years later, after seeing an advert on TV for a games software company needing new games programmers, I applied. I had to write a small game to be reviewed by the company as well as attend an interview. I got the job and haven't looked back. I'm a much better programmer now, and I'm proficient in C too, which means I'm very much more marketable when I decide to move on!'

Computer sales

In some ways, being in computer sales is one of the most important roles within the IT profession, and it is probably one of the best paid too. Computer sales staff provide business with the computer hardware, software and services they need to solve their problems and increase profitability. Whilst sales staff have an understanding of computer systems, they often rely on IT specialists to help them during the sales process, both before and after the sale (pre-sales support and post-sales support). A good knowledge of business, often in a specific field such as retail or personnel systems, is essential, as is a shrewd mind for figures. Whilst salaries for sales staff are usually high, part of the salary is usually in the form of a commission, based on the value of the sale. Many top sales staff are graduates, who can combine their technical expertise with management skills they have developed. However, there are opportunities for people from many diverse backgrounds to move into sales, maybe after performing a marketing or pre-sales support role first.

Salary
Salaries in sales can vary enormously depending on the amount of commission received. An average salary (excluding commission) could be anywhere between £30,000–£50,000, but six-figure salaries are achievable in many of the larger IT companies.

Case Study

Angela *works in the sales department for a major systems software company.*

'Although I'm in sales, my official job title is account manager – it's a bit more customer friendly than salesman (or saleswoman)! Working for a large software house whose products are written for IBM mainframe computers, I don't really need to "sell" products as such – technical support managers tend to come to me first with their problems! In my business I deal with the customer all the time, either the technical support manager, or sometimes the IT director. Whatever, they will have a clear picture of what they need from me, although they might not know of our latest piece of software which might help them. This is why I tend to bring a few technical specialists with me after the initial meeting, so they can demonstrate the product and answer any specific queries which the customer may have (apart from "How much does it cost?" – that's my job). I do understand the products from a technical point of view, as I started off as a computer programmer and then spent a few years as a team leader in a technical support environment before I eventually moved into sales. The job is very demanding; I have to travel a lot and meet customers at their convenience, not mine – so if that means meeting them at 7 pm on a Friday, then that's when I've got to go. Luckily, I enjoy meeting people and having a good chat about their specific requirements and what they've been up to recently – it all helps build rapport with the customer. The only downside is that the business lunches tend to play havoc with my figure! If I could sum up my role in one sentence, I would say "Hard work, but full of perks!"'

Technical author

It is the job of the technical author to design and produce the technical publications and documents required by people using computer systems. You might think that this task would be performed by the technical support and development staff. In some smaller companies this is probably true, but in larger companies there is usually a person with technical writing skills to perform it. A typical situation a technical author might encounter is being asked to write documentation such as:

- ◆ user guides (for people new to the computer application);
- ◆ technical reference manuals (for technicians who must support the computer systems);
- ◆ technical magazines, flysheets and any other form of written communication that contains technical information.

A technical author needs a rare set of skills, combining the roles of author and publisher with those of IT specialist. Whilst word-processing packages are widely used within the IT industry, a technical author often uses more sophisticated document-composition software, similar to the packages used within the electronic publishing industry.

Salary
Starting salaries tend to fall in the range £12,000–£15,000.

IT trainer

With the phenomenal growth in the use of IT, the role of the trainer is becoming ever more important. As more and more businesses invest in new IT systems, there is an associated need for staff to be trained to use them. Not surprisingly, IT training is an area that is expanding at a particularly fast rate compared to other occupational areas within the IT industry. Training can cover all areas of IT, such as hardware, software and networking components, but also many non-technical areas, such as report-writing and presentation skills. The scope of the training itself can vary from course to course, and can range from teaching a small group of people a few simple instructions on a PC to providing classroom-based training for a whole department on the use of a new software product.

The most important skill required for an IT trainer is to be able to communicate effectively. Basically, you must be *understood*. Obviously, you should possess good technical skills, usually in one or two main areas, but general IT skills are helpful as well. It is worth remembering that you will often present new material to the class for most of the time during a normal day, either explaining the subject to them or helping them solve any problems they might be experiencing. You need to remain calm, patient and, above all, professional at all times – not an easy job, especially when your authority might be challenged by some of the smarter students in your class!

Most companies are prepared to take on A level candidates as well as graduates, usually accepting them into some form of 'train the trainers' programme.

Further information

Lots of information on training companies, courses, qualifications and jobs can be found in specialist magazines aimed at training professionals, such as *IT Trainer*.

Salary

Starting salaries vary greatly in this area, from £16,000 for the more junior positions, to around £22,000 for new graduates.

Case Study

Michelle is a freelance trainer.

'Having worked for a number of years as a UNIX systems programmer, I realized that I actually enjoyed telling people how the computer system worked more than programming. I suspect this was partly due to the fact that I like meeting people and I consider myself to be a good communicator, especially on technical issues. For the next few years I worked in the training department of a computer vendor and enjoyed myself immensely. Not only did I have to provide a technical role in planning the course structure and content, but I also had to manage the external contractors we employed for specific courses. Recognizing the increasing demand for IT trainers, I then became a freelance contractor, giving me the freedom to train people in many other companies. Working in the M4 corridor, I am now employed by a number of major computer vendors who use freelance contractors, such as Hewlett-Packard and Sun Microsystems. The work is varied, and I do get a lot of free time between courses, which is quite nice in the demanding world of IT. If I had a dislike in being a trainer, it would be the amount of travelling I can sometimes end up doing between customer sites – still, as a contractor, my salary more than makes up for that!'

10 Getting started

Whilst this book can prepare you for a career in computing and IT, it cannot guarantee that you will be offered the first job you apply for. Even though there is currently a severe skills shortage affecting the IT industry, this is no guarantee that the skills you possess are those required by an employer. To be successful in achieving your career aims, you must plan every stage of the way. Let's 'get started' then – can you answer the following?

1. In what area of IT would you like to work (software and services, hardware, user, education, multi-media, tele-communications)?
2. What skills do you need to work in the IT area you chose in Question 1?
3. What skills do you possess – are they in demand or nearly obsolete?
4. What job role suits your current skills best?
5. Where do you want to be in five years' time?
6. Do you need to gain new skills first?
7. Is there an academic or vocational qualification you must hold for the job?
8. Is there a suitable course or government training programme that will help?
9. Where do you want to work (locally, anywhere in the UK, anywhere in the world)?
10. Where are you *able* to work – are you mobile, or must you work near where you live?

Armed with this information, you can now decide how to make your first move to help you get a job in IT. You could decide to defer writing job applications until you have gained specific skills or qualifications, as discussed later in the book, or you could decide to enter the industry straight away.

Finding a job

There are a number of sources you can use to help find a job in computing and IT. Figure 10.1 shows the main sources of information for IT job-hunters, but it is not a definitive list – you must also act on your own initiative. It is said that many IT jobs are never advertised. Why? Well, the main reason is because word has got around about the vacancy and it has been filled on the basis of personal recommendation, or by someone 'being in the right place at the right time'. Unfortunately, the IT industry is no different to any other in that sense. Whatever job you do apply for, you can be sure of one thing – many others will be applying for it too, so anything you can do to help swing things in your favour will be a worthwhile effort. Chapter 12, 'Top Tips for getting into the industry', will help you to think more about the things you can do to enhance your job-seeking prospects.

Local newspapers

Many local and national newspapers advertise vacancies for computing and IT staff, usually under the heading 'Professional' or 'Technical Appointments'. If you have restricted your job-search area to a regional area, then you will have a much better chance of finding a suitable job if you read your local papers regularly. Before you rush out and buy a copy, check which day the IT jobs are advertised. Many larger regional papers tend to have a specific day for certain types of job vacancy. For instance, the *Manchester Evening News* advertises computing and IT vacancies on a Thursday.

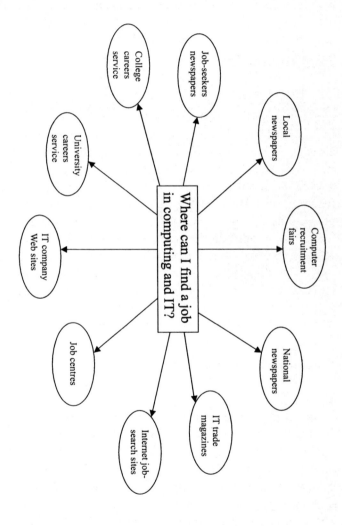

Figure 10.1 Where to find a job in computing and IT

National newspapers

Whilst the national daily newspapers generally advertise more computing and IT jobs than their local counterparts, these jobs are primarily aimed at graduates and those IT professionals seeking a more senior role. As you would expect, national newspapers advertise national computing and IT vacancies to be found all over the UK, and in many cases they advertise jobs in other countries too. The majority of IT jobs in the UK, however, are still to be found in south-east England. Figure 10.2 gives you an idea of how the majority of IT companies are distributed throughout the UK and Eire.

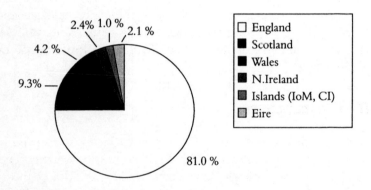

Figure 10.2 The distribution of IT sites within the UK and Eire

Table 10.1 should help you plan which national newspapers to read and when to read them.

Table 10.1   IT jobs advertised in national newspapers

Newspaper	Advertises IT jobs on:
Guardian	Thursday
Daily Telegraph/Sunday Telegraph	Thursday, Saturday, Sunday
The Times/Sunday Times	Thursday, Sunday

Specialist 'job-seekers' newspapers

Often published weekly, these large-format newspapers are full of jobs and careers advice, usually for a particular region of the UK (*Yorkshire Jobs*, for instance). Whilst general in nature and catering for many different professions, they are categorized quite well. IT jobs appear under headings such as 'Technical', 'Professional' or 'Computing'.

IT trade magazines

With an industry as diverse as IT, it is not a complete surprise to find a large number of both general and specialist magazines published specifically for the IT professional. Not all of these, however, include appointments sections, but it is worth paying a visit to the library to have a read of them all the same. The main two magazines that contain advertisements (as well as lots of other useful information, technical articles and news) are *Computing* and *Computer Weekly*. Both are well-established and pride themselves on the staggering number of IT vacancies they publish. They are free to people working in the IT industry, or you can buy them at most newsagents or read them at most libraries.

Recruitment and information magazines

Computing

VNU Business Publications
VNU House
32–34 Broadwick Street
London W1A 2HG
Tel: (020) 7316 9000
Web site: www.computing.co.uk

Computer Weekly
Reed Business Publishing
Quadrant House
The Quadrant
Sutton
Surrey SM2 5AS
Tel: (01444) 441212
Web site: www.computerweekly.co.uk

Network News
VNU Business Publications
VNU House
32–34 Broadwick Street
London W1A 2HG
Tel: (020) 7316 9000
Web site: www.networknews.co.uk

General interest magazines

Internet Business

Haymarket Management Publications Ltd
174 Hammersmith Road
London W6 7JP
Tel: (020) 8267 4625
Web site: www.ibmag.co.uk

PC Home, PC Advisor, Windows Expert, PC Basics
IDG Media
Media House
Adlington Park
Macclesfield
Cheshire SK10 4NP
Tel: (01625) 87888

Accessing job vacancies from the Internet

Using the Internet, you can access the World Wide Web and download information on IT vacancies in the UK and throughout the world. You can also read hundreds of helpful articles on the latest technologies, issues and general career advice. Most people access the Internet either at work, at university or at home (if they have a PC, modem and Internet connection software). Alternatively, most libraries now have PCs connected to the Internet.

Many companies that use IT have a Web site you can connect to if you know their address on the World Wide Web (www). From their Web site you can find information about the company, including vacancies and recruitment procedures. For example, Cap Gemini, the IT services company, has a Web site address of: www.capgemini.co.uk. An excellent book on how to use the Web to help develop your career and find work has been published by Kogan Page (the publishers of this book). *Net That Job!* by Irene Krechowiecka is full of information and Web site addresses that will help you develop a career in IT; it is well worth reading.

Registering with an IT recruitment agency

The current skills shortage in the IT profession is generating huge amounts of work for the specialist IT recruitment agencies, whose main objective is to match their registered clients with vacancies from the IT companies they help. Although all IT companies have personnel departments, they often use recruitment agencies to advertise vacancies and perform selection interviews on their behalf, because they do not have the time to handle the hundreds of (often unsuitable) applications they would otherwise receive.

Agencies are very popular with many IT professionals, as they are extremely good at getting them a large number of interviews in a relatively short space of time. Agencies work on a commission basis, receiving payment from the recruiting company, usually for every candidate sent for interview plus a bonus payment should the candidate accept the position (usually a percentage of the salary). You may be wondering why I am telling you how agencies earn a living. It is because doing so should highlight the main problem with using recruitment agencies – whilst they will bend over backwards to find you work if you possess real skills and experience in key areas, they will soon lose interest in you if you cannot offer them the skills they are seeking. Many of these agencies employ highly skilled, sincere professionals, who will gladly offer career advice and guidance – but they are not a charity. Nevertheless, because of the skills shortage, many agencies are now looking for IT graduates straight from university as well as experienced professionals (minimum six months' experience is expected). Lists of specialist computer recruitment agencies can be found in *Computing* and *Computer Weekly*, or in the *Yellow Pages*, listed under 'Employment Agencies'.

Approaching employers directly

Whilst it is all very well taking the initiative and contacting employers directly, studies have suggested it is really not worth doing unless you have inside knowledge of a vacancy that has not yet been advertised or know someone within the organization who will help with your application.

In one study, over 80 per cent of test applicants who applied directly to the employer were politely informed that 'there are no vacancies at the present time, but your details will be kept on file'. When the employers were asked three months later about the application details filed, they admitted they did not really have time to sift through any of the applications in the file, apart from those received in response to a specific advertisement.

If you are confident you *can* bypass the normal recruitment process, then write a short, simple letter to the IT recruitment manager (or personnel manager), explaining your skills and interests, preferably enclosing a copy of your Curriculum Vitae (or CV, as it is more commonly known). If possible, find out the name of this manager and address your letter accordingly – it usually guarantees someone will at least read it. The following points are worth heeding when writing a speculative letter to an employer for any IT vacancy:

- type your letter (or use a word processor) on good quality white A4 paper;
- briefly describe your skills and experience in one paragraph (the rest is on your CV);
- state your availability for an informal discussion or interview;
- leave a contact address and phone number;
- always enclose an SAE for reply.

Further information
Details of IT companies, including contact addresses and the software and hardware they use, can be found in *The Computer Users Year Book*, usually available from the reference section of most libraries.

Writing a successful CV

Sooner or later, there comes a time when you need to respond to a job advertisement, not only by writing a letter of application, saying why you would like the job, but also by sending a current copy of your Curriculum Vitae. 'Curriculum Vitae' comes from the Latin and means 'the way your life has run'. It has just one main purpose – to get you an interview with your employer. In other words, it must sell you (and your skills) to the employer in about 20 seconds, because that is the average time spent reading one! Writing a CV (and keeping it up to date) is something you should take very seriously, as it is often the only weapon you have in getting past the front door of many personnel departments. With this point in mind, I suggest you read the following book: *Preparing Your Own CV* by Rebecca Corfield, published by Kogan Page (1999).

Who will employ me?

There are literally hundreds of employers throughout the UK seeking people with IT skills; listing them all would warrant a book in its own right! Whilst it is good practice to read the IT trade magazines mentioned within this chapter for names of IT companies and agencies, many people like to know the names of at least a few of the larger organizations when they are thinking about applying for a job.

To get you started, here is a list of some of the leading IT employers in the UK. A brief introductory letter or telephone call to any one of these may help you get started. All the following companies participate in the British Computer Society's Professional Development Scheme:

Avesta Sheffield Ltd
BOC Group
Britannia Building Society
British Gas Transco
British Nuclear Fuels Ltd – IT Services
BT Networks and Systems
Cap Gemini UK plc
Charles Schwab Europe
Cornwall District Council
Defence Research Agency
Essex County Council
Ford Motor Company
HM Land Registry
ICL
Lloyd's Register
London Borough of Camden
Manchester Metropolitan University
National Power plc
NATS Software Services
Oxford Radcliffe Hospital
PA Consulting Group
Post Office IT Services
Reuters Ltd
Royal & Sun Alliance

Scottish Executive
South East London Health
University of Wales Swansea
Vodafone Group plc
Which?

Employers in Northern Ireland

Despite the majority of IT sites being within England, there are a great many IT companies that are located in Northern Ireland, many of which are large international software and services companies. *The Computer Users Year Book* ('IT Sites' supplement), available from main libraries, provides information on IT sites throughout the UK and Eire. Alternatively, details of hardware, software and IT consultancy companies based in Northern Ireland can be found on the Web site: www.guide-to-nireland.com.

A few of the larger companies worth investigating include:

BIC Systems Ltd
Bull Information Systems
CFM Systems
Computastore
Coopers & Lybrand
Data General Ltd
Digital Equipment Company Ltd
How Systems Ltd
IBM (UK) Ltd
ICL (UK) Ltd
KPMG Peat Marwick
Lagan Technologies Ltd
McDonnell Information Systems (MDIS)
Nezz Networking
Nortel (Northern Telecom)
Parity Solutions (Ireland) Ltd
Real Time Systems Ltd
Siemens Nixdorf Information Systems
Vision Information Consulting
Zaray Internet Consultants

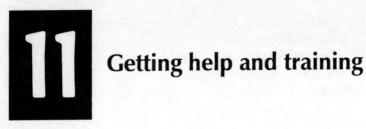

11 Getting help and training

The graduate and A level induction programmes are a welcome introduction into computing and IT for many students, but what about everyone else? Luckily, there are a number of organizations that can find you work and training in IT, regardless of your educational qualifications or financial status. With the current skills shortage in IT, employers are as keen to find suitable employees as you are to find work, so use this to your advantage. Figure 11.1 (see page 104) highlights the main sources of help and training you can use.

Using the Careers Service

If you are currently at school, college or university, then you have probably been introduced to the Careers Service already. If not, then there are a number of careers offices scattered around the country, which offer the same service. You can find your nearest careers office by looking in the *Yellow Pages* under 'Careers'. Whilst the Careers Service does not specialize in any one particular employment area, it is fully aware of opportunities within the IT industry. Having links with training organizations as well as business, the Careers Service can provide the following services:

◆ a list of computing vacancies within the area;
◆ advice on training organizations (colleges, universities and government-backed training companies) that can help you gain the necessary skills;

- advice on studying for qualifications whilst in work (vocational qualifications);
- information on local and national employers;
- help with recruitment and selection procedures, such as computer aptitude tests.

Using the Job Centre

Job Centres are situated in most towns and cities and are a prime source of help and advice for anyone seeking employment. Most people view Job Centres as rather depressing places, which only advertise vacancies for low-paid and unskilled jobs. This is not the case. Job Centres regularly advertise professional and technical employment opportunities within computing and IT, mainly locally, but sometimes nationally or even internationally. For people seeking employment specifically within IT, Job Centres can provide the following services:

- Notice of current or forthcoming IT vacancies.
- A free Executive Recruitment Service, designed to match professional people with suitable vacancies in the IT sector.
- A free Employment Service Programme giving advice on applying for jobs, writing CVs and interview techniques.
- Access to the 'Job Club' service, which gives entitled individuals access to a wide range of resources to help them find and apply for jobs, such as newspapers, stamps, word-processing and printing facilities.
- Advice on vocational training and other facilities offered by the Training and Enterprise Council.
- Computer-based Training Access Points (TAPs) that are easy-to-use large-scale computer screens designed to give people information on local training and education opportunities. Whilst they are for general use, there is a section on computing and IT. TAPs can also be found in many libraries.
- Leaflets, books and periodicals on a wide range of areas, such as job vacancies, training, qualifications and employment case studies.

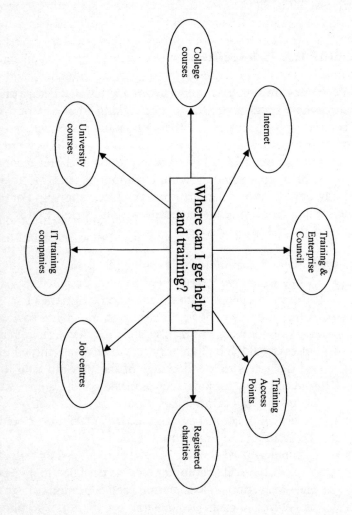

Figure 11.1 Where to go for help and training

IT training companies

All of the major computer vendors and training companies run in-house courses, covering a wide range of topics on many different platforms. As you would expect, the standard of the tuition is extremely high and, as many courses provide 'hands-on' experience in the classroom, these courses are very popular amongst IT professionals. Before you attend one of these courses you should think very seriously about the cost – they are not cheap and you may find a similar course, costing considerably less, being run at a local college or university.

Commercial training companies

The following companies are just a few of the many training organizations that provide a wide range of training programmes, covering all aspects of computing and IT. In addition, many also run non-technical courses, such as communication skills and team-building skills courses.

Amdahl UK Education
Beaumont
Old Windsor
Berkshire SL4 2JP
Tel: (01753) 833555
IBM Education
Tel: 0345 581329

Learning Tree International
Learning Tree International Ltd
Mole Business Park
Leatherhead
Surrey KT22 7AD
Tel: (01372) 364610 or 0800 282353

Microsoft Education
For training in all Microsoft products and MCPS/MCSE certification. Microsoft have a large number of Approved Training Centres where you can obtain training throughout the UK. Contact:
Microsoft Limited
Microsoft Place
Winnersh
Wokingham
Berkshire RG41 5TP
Training hotline: 0345 000111

Novell UK Education and Training
For all Novell courses including CNA and CNE certification.
Tel: 0800 966196

Oracle Education
For training on all Oracle products and general IT skills.
Tel: (01344) 383755

Sun Microsystems Ltd
Educational Services
Watchmoor Park
Riverside Way
Camberley
Surrey GU15 3YL
Tel: (01276) 416520

The role of the Training and Enterprise Council

More commonly known as the TEC, the Training and Enterprise Council is an organization contracted by the Department for Education and Employment to administer and co-ordinate a number of Youth Training Schemes throughout the UK. There are currently 82 TECs, or Local Enterprise Companies in Scotland (LECs), which operate within strict regional boundaries based on postcode. All TECs and LECs share the same objective – to provide training opportunities for the 16-plus age group. For instance, if you are a college student and you need to attend a specific IT exhibition or training seminar, the TEC can fund the cost. TECs are also key players in the Learning Card Scheme, which is available to school and college leavers. Through this scheme (which might be known by another name in your area) you can access a number of training schemes, such as the Modern Apprenticeship and National Traineeship programmes, which can lead to a recognized National Vocational Qualification (NVQ) in information technology. Further details on NVQs and Modern Apprenticeships can be found in Chapter 14. To find your local TEC, look in the telephone directory under 'Training'.

For more general information on training opportunities contact Partnerships, Skills and Young People Division, Department for Education and Employment, Room W4d, Moorfoot, Sheffield S1 4PQ (tel: 0114 259 3573).

12 Top Tips for getting into the industry

◆ Be able to *demonstrate* your skills or experience. Have you written a program to solve a problem or fixed a PC either at home or in college? Any practical experience is worth its weight in gold.

◆ Talk to the employers. They need staff as much as you need a job. Ask personnel or human resources managers what skills or qualifications they expect potential employees to possess. Showing initiative often creates opportunity.

◆ Many employers want IT staff to have a broad understanding of *all* the issues affecting IT. Reading IT trade magazines helps boost your knowledge. Understanding general IT issues also prepares you for tricky interview questions, such as 'How do you think we can make use of the Internet?'

◆ Be flexible and open-minded. Seek opportunity. If you are offered a job in IT that is not the one you hoped for, it might be worth taking it to gain experience. See if you can transfer between teams at a later stage or go on a suitable training course.

◆ Remember the skills shortage. Try to identify an area where you could fit in quickly; determine what skills you need and aim to satisfy them.

◆ Be patient – the IT industry will still be here tomorrow. If you need to do a three-year degree course to achieve your career goal, do it.

♦ Get as much hands-on experience as you can. PCs are com-
monplace now – try to get hold of one if possible and teach
yourself the basic skills. The Internet is a good example –
you can teach yourself the basics of Web design. Many of
the skills currently in demand are PC-based and can be
learnt at home, such as Visual Basic, C++ and Microsoft
Office.

♦ There are numerous CD ROM-based training books and
manuals to help you gain new skills, many being commonly used within the IT industry. Don't buy them; most
libraries now stock IT training materials.

13

The future of computing and information technology

Following the completion of many year 2000 conversion projects (often at considerable cost to business), it might have been thought that the business community would treat itself to a well-earned break from IT. However, the business world cannot afford to ignore IT for too long. Even the most traditional company directors now reluctantly agree that their business can only grow by taking advantage of new IT developments, such as electronic commerce and super-fast digital networks (the 'information super-highway', as it is often called).

Many people may be unaware of one key event that took place during 1999, when a number of European countries agreed to adopt the euro as their new 'single' currency. In IT terms, the level of change (and therefore risk) was huge, but the project was a resounding success. However, full European monetary union is still a long way off, and much has to be done, both politically and technically, to ensure its future success.

You may already have noticed a new symbol on your PC keyboard, the € symbol, a simple but necessary change to allow us to refer to the euro within our electronic documents and presentations. Unfortunately, in the complex world of computing and IT, nothing is quite that simple. For instance, how will countries that have not yet joined the European single currency (such as the UK) trade if their ordering and purchasing systems do not currently allow them to trade in euros? How will the computer systems of mortgage lenders cope with people wanting to buy a house using euros? How will countries outside Europe trade with countries adopting this currency?

All the time, thousands of monetary transactions take place between the UK, the rest of Europe and, indeed, the rest of the world. Changing the very currency they use in their calculations will give many businesses a big headache, being in some ways a greater problem than the year 2000 was. This suggests there will be big demands placed on IT professionals to renovate the systems – and that means lots of jobs.

The growth of the Internet into a reliable and cheap technology that can successfully compete with traditional forms of business is still a few years away, but the signs are looking promising. Most companies have now realized the importance of having a Web site, which in effect is their 'electronic shop window'. Not only will they have to compete for business on the high street, but they will also have to compete with other companies advertising their products and services on the World Wide Web.

This new wave of electronic commerce (e-commerce) has given rise to a new business phrase, the 'Martini Syndrome', meaning that electronic forms of business can take place 'any time, any place, anywhere' (if you are old enough to remember the popular drink advert). Soon, it is hoped, the Internet will become a fast and reliable way of communicating, and as simple as picking up the telephone for placing an order.

Microchips are getting smaller and can be fitted virtually anywhere, from the fridge at home to a car dashboard. IBM now has a 1-inch square disk that can process the same amount of information as a laptop. Along with the developments in mobile phone technology and the expansion of interactive digital TV, this heralds a new era in communications and, ultimately, business. By 2010, it is predicted that two-thirds of all e-commerce will originate from something other than a PC – one-third from interactive TV and one-third from over the telephone.

Computing and IT has come a long way since being introduced nearly 50 years ago. It is almost impossible to imagine that the average home PC is massively more powerful than the very first computer, which filled a ground-floor laboratory. If this rate of change continues, then who knows what computing and IT will offer in 50 years' time – we all have an exciting future.

14 What qualifications will I need?

Whilst many successful careers have been built around experience alone, there are a number of good reasons for obtaining an IT-related qualification:

◆ meeting membership criteria for professional IT bodies such as the British Computer Society;
◆ to gain accelerated promotion into senior positions;
◆ as a 'passport' for moving between IT jobs.

Of course, professional qualifications on their own do not guarantee success – training and experience are also needed in many areas – but there is no doubt that a computing qualification provides a potential employer with a recognized assessment of level of commitment and competence.

As well as gaining academic skills, courses such as degrees and higher diplomas can also provide you with many of the 'soft' skills that are highly sought after in industry, such as team-working and project management.

The main IT qualifications available are:

◆ National Traineeship;
◆ Modern Apprenticeship;
◆ GNVQ Intermediate or Advanced;
◆ A levels;
◆ BTEC HNC or HND;
◆ NVQ in IT;

- degree;
- recognized qualifications from IT training companies.

National Traineeships

A National Traineeship is a work-based training programme leading to at least an NVQ 2 and Key Skills. Being a work-based qualification, you also receive a wage whilst you train. National Traineeships can last up to two years, depending on how much you know before you start, how hard you work, and how much help you get from your employer.

To become a National Trainee you will be:

- aged between 16 and 19;
- interested in a career in computing and IT;
- able to work and study at the same time;
- able to demonstrate a potential to achieve NVQ 2 and Key Skills.

A National Traineeship can lead to:

- entry on to a Modern Apprenticeship scheme;
- more work experience and an HNC;
- gaining an NVQ 3 whilst at work.

Modern Apprenticeships

A Modern Apprenticeship is a work-based training programme that leads to the achievement of an NVQ 3 and Key Skills. Whilst it is a training programme, it is also a job, and a Modern Apprentice is paid whilst training. The Modern Apprenticeship in IT has three routes:

- using IT;
- operating, installing and supporting IT systems;
- developing IT systems.

A Modern Apprenticeship takes up to three years to complete but, as with the National Traineeship, you can reduce the time needed in a number of ways.

To become a Modern Apprentice you will be:

◆ aged between 16 and 19;
◆ interested in a career in computing and IT;
◆ able to work and study at the same time;
◆ able to demonstrate the potential to achieve NVQ 3 and Key Skills.

A Modern Apprenticeship can lead to:

◆ entry on to a degree;
◆ entry on to an HND;
◆ gaining an NVQ 4 in IT.

Business and Technology Education Council (BTEC) Certificates and Diplomas

BTEC qualifications are recognized nationally in England, Wales and Northern Ireland and in some countries overseas. Being vocational in nature they tend to offer practical computing skills rather than academic theory and are widely respected for their relevance to computing occupations within the IT industry. BTEC qualifications are considered equivalent to A levels and are normally accepted by universities for entry on to a degree programme. In Scotland, the role of BTEC is performed by the Scottish Qualifications Authority (SQA).

The main BTEC qualifications available are:

◆ First Certificate/Diploma – age on entry 16-plus; one-year course; equivalent to two GCSEs at grades A–C*; leads to A levels, BTEC National qualification and NVQ level 3.
◆ Advanced GNVQ (General NVQ) – no formal entry requirements; normally a two-year course, but no real time constraints; equivalent to two A levels.*

◆ National Certificate/Diploma – no formal entry requirements; three-year part-time or two-year full-time course;
equivalent to two A levels.*
◆ Higher National Certificate/Diploma – no formal entry
requirements, but either of the following indicates suitabil-
ity: one A level or BTEC National qualification; equivalent
to a degree.*

* Owing to the vocational nature of BTEC programmes, a
direct comparison is not always appropriate. These, however,
are the generally accepted equivalents.

University degrees

There is now a wide variety of computing degrees available from
universities, which go some way beyond the 'standard' computer
science degree, reflecting the importance the industry is placing
on new technologies. For example, degrees such as artificial intelligence, cybernetics and software engineering are available, which
qualify you for work within the more specialized fields of the IT
industry.

In England, Wales and Northern Ireland, degrees normally
comprise three years' full-time study, or four years' study including a year's placement in industry (a 'sandwich' degree). Remembering that employers are looking for practical skills as well as
academic knowledge, a year spent in industry attracts the attention
of many IT recruitment managers, and can often mean a larger
starting salary.

Whilst entry to higher education can be achieved through
courses such as BTEC National Certificates and Diplomas,
GNVQ Advanced and Modern Apprenticeships, the most popular route to university is by taking A levels. With one or two A levels, you can usually apply for an ordinary degree, but three A levels
are normally expected for honours degrees. You do not need
mathematics or computing A levels, but you do need to get the
highest grades you can, as competition for popular degrees is
fierce. If, however, you decide to study for a scientific degree, such

as computational mathematics or cybernetics, you will normally be expected to have good A level grades in mathematics or physics.

National Vocational Qualifications

National Vocational Qualifications (NVQs, or SVQs in Scotland) in computing and IT are a new and flourishing framework of nationally recognized awards that have been jointly developed by the IT profession and the National Training Organization for IT (ITNTO).

The main aim of an IT NVQ is to provide people with skills that are used and recognized by the IT industry, by adopting a more practical approach to training. Each award is made up of a series of work units that relate to the NVQ topic; the number of units studied for is dependent upon the level of NVQ. There are five levels of NVQ:

- NVQ level 1 provides basic skills, roughly equivalent to GCSEs.
- NVQ level 2 builds on skills and develops greater understanding.
- NVQ level 3 assumes more responsibility in the role (equivalent to A levels).
- NVQ levels 4 and 5 provide a professional (degree standard) and postgraduate level of understanding.

Why should I consider an NVQ?

Reasons for considering an NVQ are as follows:

- Not everyone is comfortable sitting exams. NVQs assess your competence at work and rarely involve sitting exams.
- They relate to the real word, which is a great advantage.
- NVQs are flexible. There are no time limits, no age limits and no special entry requirements.

NVQs in computing and IT are offered by many colleges and training institutions throughout the UK, and are awarded by a number of examinations bodies, which all offer their own IT NVQ. For example, the following NVQs are awarded by the City & Guilds of London Institute:

- using information technology;
- use and support of information technology;
- operating information technology;
- software creation;
- install information technology products;
- support users of information technology;
- information systems analysis;
- information systems design and programming;
- implement information technology solutions.

Further information
For more information on the NVQ framework, contact:

- IT employers (they might operate NVQ schemes);
- your local college of further education;
- the Job Centre;
- the Training and Enterprise Council (TEC).

Alternatively, contact The National Council for Vocational Qualifications (NCVQ), Customer Services, NCVQ, 222 Euston Road, London NW1 2BZ (tel: 0171 728 1914).

Recognized qualifications from IT training companies

City & Guilds Basic Certificate in computer programming

The City & Guilds (C&G) Institute awards a number of qualifications, which are widely recognized and appreciated by IT employers. The C&G Certificate in computer programming is a popular choice for many people who want to enter the IT profession directly (or straight from school) as a trainee or junior programmer. Most of the courses offered by the C&G Institute require no formal entry qualifications, although it is better if you do possess GCSE English language and mathematics (or the equivalent).

Royal Society of Arts qualifications

Founded in 1754, the Royal Society of Arts (RSA) provides a number of qualifications covering IT in general as well as specific IT applications. RSA programmes are offered by approved centres, which can be training institutions or colleges of further education. Main RSA qualifications include computer literacy and information technology (CLAIT), and integrated business technology stage II. CLAIT is a popular, flexible course in IT, which is taken annually by more than 120,000 candidates, 40 per cent of whom are schoolchildren. CLAIT is an employable qualification in its own right, but also provides a solid grounding for further study, such as GNVQ, NVQ or A level. Integrated business technology stage II is a more advanced course, which integrates a number of IT applications in a simulated office situation, requiring some knowledge of hardware. To enrol, you need skills at least to CLAIT level.

Vendor-specific qualifications

In the pursuit of gaining highly productive staff very quickly, some employers now prefer applicants with specific qualifications in IT software and hardware as opposed to the more generic IT qualifications available in colleges and universities. Vendor-specific qualifications are becoming as important as degrees and diplomas with many companies, as they certify competency in a product in a way that is recognized throughout the world.

The leading vendor-specific qualifications are:

◆ Certified Novell Administrator (CNA) – to handle day-to-day administration of an installed Novell networking product, such as Netware.

- Certified Novell Engineer (CNE) – for installing and upgrading network systems and performing tuning.
- Microsoft Certified Product Specialist (MCPS) – qualified to install, configure and support Microsoft desktop products. MCPSs have considerable knowledge in one of the Microsoft operating systems.
- Microsoft Certified Systems Engineer (MCSE) – qualified to install and support Windows NT and server products. Candidates must pass a total of six exams to achieve certification.
- Certified Java Programmer – to gain knowledge in basic Java programming techniques.
- Certified Java Developer – for more in-depth knowledge of Java, including memory management, screen design and graphics. To gain this qualification you must first possess the Certified Java Programmer qualification.

15 Where to study

University courses

For details of all university courses and entrance requirements, consult the *UCAS Handbook*. For all matters concerning university admission and student loans contact Universities and Colleges Admissions Service, Fulton House, Jessop Avenue, Cheltenham, Gloucestershire GL50 3SH (tel: 01242 227788).

Open University degrees

The Open University (OU) specializes in offering a wide range of courses (including degrees) that are completed at home. To obtain an OU degree, you need to accumulate credits in core and supplementary modules over a number of years. For more information on the Open University contact The Open University, Central Enquiry Service, PO Box 200, Walton Hall, Milton Keynes MK7 6YZ (tel: 01908 653231).

College courses

Many colleges now offer good full-time, part-time or evening classes, which are often cheap and sometimes free. For details of colleges offering A levels, C&G/RSA awards, GNVQs, NVQs and BTECs, use a TAP, visit your TEC or read the following:

CRAC Directory of Further Education, published by Hobsons Publishing plc, available in the reference section of most libraries.

City & Guilds of London Institute study centres

For details of examinations and approved study centres contact City & Guilds of London Institute, 1 Giltspur Street, London EC1A 9DD (tel: 020 7294 2468).

Centres offering National Vocational Qualifications

For details of colleges and training establishments offering NVQs in IT, you must first contact one of the NVQ awarding bodies. All of the following organizations award NVQs in IT and can provide details of courses and places to study:

British Computer Society
1 Sandford Street
Swindon SN1 1HJ
Tel: (01793) 417147

Business and Technology Education Council
Upper Woburn Place
Central House
London WC1H 0HH
Tel: (020) 7413 8400

City & Guilds of London Institute
1 Giltspur Street
London EC1A 9DD
Tel: (020) 7294 2468

City & Guilds Scotland
22 Walker Street
Edinburgh EH3 7HR
Tel: (0131) 226 1556

London Chamber of Commerce and Industry (LCCI)
Marlow House
Station Road
Sidcup
Kent DA5 7BJ
Tel: (020) 8302 0261

National Computing Centre
Oxford House
Oxford Road
Manchester M1 7ED
Tel: (0161) 228 6333

National Computing Centre Scotland
Anderson House
389 Argyle Street
Glasgow G2 8LF
Tel: (0141) 204 3725

Pitman Examinations Institute
1 Giltspur Street
London EC1A 9DD
Tel: (020) 7294 2471

RSA Examinations Board
Westwood Way
Coventry CV4 8HS
Tel: (024) 76470033

Scottish Qualifications Agency
Hanover House
24 Douglas Street
Glasgow G2 7NQ
Tel: (0141) 248 7900

Telecommunications Vocational Standards Council
Blackfriars House
339 South Row
Central Milton Keynes MK9 2PG
Tel: (01908) 20120

16 Useful addresses

IT professional bodies

The British Computer Society (BCS)
1 Sandford Street
Swindon SN1 1HJ
Tel: (01793) 417417

The Council of European Professional Informatics Societies
 (CEPIS)
7 Mansfield Mews
London W1M 9FJ
Tel: (020) 7637 5607

The Engineering Council
10 Maltravers Street
London WC2R 3ER
Tel: (020) 7240 7891

The Institute of Data Processing Management (IDPM)
IDPM House
Edgington Way
Ruxley Corner
Sidcup
Kent DA14 5HR
Tel: (020) 8308 0747

17 Further reading

Job hunting

Byron, M (1994) *How To Pass Graduate Recruitment Tests*, Kogan Page
Corfield, R (1999) *Successful Interview Skills*, Kogan Page
Krechowiecka, I (1998) *Net That Job!*, Kogan Page
Modha, S (1994) *How To Pass Computer Selection Tests*, Kogan Page

Teaching

Taylor, F (1997) *Careers in Teaching*, Kogan Page

Education and qualifications

British Qualifications (1995) Kogan Page
British Vocational Qualifications (1995) Kogan Page
Sponsorship for Students, published and distributed by the Careers Research Advisory Centre (CRAC) and Hobsons Publishing plc. Contains 2,500 scholarships and bursaries from 200 different organizations. Copies are available from Customer Services REF F30, Biblios PDS Ltd, Star Road, Partridge Green, West Sussex RH13 8LD (tel: 01403 710851).

Employment opportunities

Considering Computer Contracting
Freelance Year Book
Getting Computer Jobs Abroad

All published by Computer Weekly Publications, PO Box 935, Finchingfield, Braintree, Essex CM7 4LN (tel: 0371 811160).

Useful books on computing and IT

General

Maran, R (1998) *Teach Yourself Computers & the Internet Visually*, IDG
White, R (1999) *How Computers Work: Millennium edition*, Que

PC

Mueller, S (1999) *Upgrading and Repairing PCs*, Que
Rathbone, A (1998) *Upgrading and Fixing PCs for Dummies*, IDG Books

The Internet

Bride, M (1999) *How to Use the Internet*, Hodder & Stoughton
Kent, P (1998) *The Complete Idiot's Guide to the Internet*, Que

Game design

De Goes, J (1999) *3D Game Programming with C++*, Coriolis Group Books
Saltzman, M (1999) *Game Design: Secrets of the sages*, Brady Publishing

Popular operating systems

Bott, E and Person, R (1998) *Using Windows 95 (Special Edition)*, Que
Levine, J and Young, M (1998) *Unix for Dummies*, IDG Books
Rathbone, A (1997) *Windows 95 for Dummies*, IDG Books
Wagner, B (1998) *The Complete Idiot's Guide to UNIX*, Que

Programming languages

Davis, S (1998) *C++ for Dummies*, IDG Books
Gookin, D (1994) *C for Dummies*, IDG Books

Oracle database software

Oracle: A Beginner's Guide (1995)
Oracle DBA Handbook (7.3 Edition) (1997)
Oracle: Developer/2000 Handbook (1997)
Oracle: The Complete Reference (Electronic Edition) (1997)

All published by Osborne/McGraw-Hill, and also available from
Oracle (tel: 0990 997788 and ask for bookshop).

Networking

Derfler, F and Free, L (1998) *How Networks Work*, Que
Nance, B (1997) *Introduction to Networking*, Que

Systems development methodologies

Weaver, P L (1998) *Practical SSADM Version 4*, Financial Times
Management

Computer training videos and software

Many libraries now stock computer training videos, covering subjects such as Microsoft Office, UNIX and Visual Basic.

A huge selection of computer manuals, computer-based training packages, CD ROMs and videos is available from most Internet bookshops (such as www.amazon.co.uk or alternatively from Computer Manuals Ltd, 28 Lincoln Road, Olton, Birmingham B27 6PA (tel: 0121 706 6000; Web site: www.computer-manuals.co.uk).

Glossary

artificial intelligence (AI) Computer systems that perform human functions that would normally require intelligence, eg reasoning and decision-making.

Assembler A low-level programming language that can be converted into machine code. Assembler language is often used for applications where speed is important, such as games programming.

bridge A device that connects two networks together.

business process re-engineering Radically improving the business by using IT to improve performance and cut costs.

C A high-level programming language developed at Bell Laboratories (US). UNIX is written in C.

C++ A more advanced version of the C programming language, which is used for object-orientated program development.

CD ROM Compact disc read-only memory. A small plastic disc that is used as a high-capacity storage device. A CD ROM player is the device that enables a computer to read the CD ROM.

client-server architecture A network of computers in which a central (server) computer carries out tasks in response to instructions from other computers (clients) in the network.

COBOL Common ordinary business-oriented language. An old but very popular programming language used for writing business applications.

console A computer terminal that allows a computer operator to access the computer system, usually in order to issue operating system commands.

CPU Central processing unit. The computing part of a computer, contained on a single chip.

database A set of related files, which can store text, images, sound and video. Traditionally, databases are used where users need access to large amounts of information, as in stock-control systems or customer account databases.

distributed computing Sharing many computers that are connected together over a network.

DVD Digital versatile disc. Originally called the digital videodisc, a DVD is a type of optical disc similar to a CD, but capable of storing much more information. DVD technology is used by the film industry to store video information and is expected eventually to replace video tapes.

Ethernet A local area network protocol (a set of rules that determine how data should be transmitted and received across a LAN).

expert system Software that applies the knowledge of a human expert in a particular field to help diagnose problems.

gateway A device used to link two different types of network together, eg a LAN and a WAN.

high-level language A programming language that allows the programmer to write programs using English-like statements (as in COBOL). A separate operation is then performed to translate the program into instructions the computer will understand.

HTML HyperText Markup Language. The document format used on the World Wide Web. Web pages that can be downloaded from the Web are written in HTML.

interactive TV Sometimes called 'Web TV'. Allows two-way communication between the viewer and the provider of the service. Now used to describe 'Internet TV', which involves a 'set-top box' and a modem, allowing the user to access the Internet via the TV.

Internet An international wide area network connecting together many local networks, which provides electronic mail and file transfer facilities.

intranet A term given to a local or secure Internet, eg a network that exists within a company for use by its employees.

Jackson Structured Programming (JSP) A popular method of writing and designing structured computer programs, developed by Michael Jackson.
Java A high-level computer programming language developed by Sun for writing Internet and intranet applications.

LAN Local area network. A system of computer terminals and devices connected together within a short distance of each other, eg a series of PCs linked together in the IT department of an organization.

microchip An electronic circuit used in the assembly of micro-computers, etched on to a silicon semiconductor (or 'chip').
mid-range computer A medium-sized computer system or server.
modem A device that allows computer data to be transmitted over telephone lines.
monitor A visual display unit (VDU) used to display high-quality text and graphics on a computer.
MVS Multiple Virtual Storage. A popular (and very powerful) IBM mainframe operating system.

online Connected to and under the control of a computer; available for immediate use. For example, if you connect to the Internet, you are online when you make the connection to the modem and provide a user name and password.
operating system A series of programs that control the basic functions of a computer system, such as input/output, memory allocation and file-handling.

PC Personal computer. A general term relating to a microcomputer having an Intel processor based on the IBM PC-style architecture.
pseudo-code English-like sentences that are used in program design to describe the operation of the program.

real-time A computer system that processes events as they happen, allowing decisions to be made that could influence those events (eg a missile guidance system).

RISC Reduced instruction set computer. A computer architecture that reduces chip complexity by using simpler instructions.

router A communications device that accepts data and forwards it on to its destination using the most efficient route through a network.

scanner A device that reads a printed page and converts it into a digital image on a computer.

search engine Software that searches for data based on certain criteria, now used extensively throughout the World Wide Web. Web Crawler is a popular Internet search engine.

server A computer on a network that provides services used by other computers in the network.

software engineering A computing field covering all aspects of software development. Software engineering taught in universities often relates to the *science* of writing and testing programs.

SSADM A popular systems development methodology.

terminal A device consisting of a visual display unit and a keyboard, which provides access to a computer system.

token ring A popular type of LAN architecture in which a computer connected to it can only transmit data when it is in possession of a token.

transaction A general term usually relating to any single action that is performed against a database (eg deleting a record).

UNIX A popular multi-user operating system developed by AT&T Bell Laboratories, which runs on almost any computer from a PC to a mainframe.

virus A program that attaches to a computer system and then spreads itself to other files or computers on the network, often corrupting them in the process.

Visual Basic A popular PC-based programming language.

WAN A network that connects computers over large distances, using high-speed telephone lines, radio and satellites.

Web browser The program that serves as your front end to the World Wide Web on the Internet. In order to access a Web site, the address of the site (such as www. bbc.co.uk) is entered in the location field of the browser and the site's 'home' Web page is downloaded.

Windows A popular family of operating systems developed by the Microsoft Corporation for use on PCs.

World Wide Web An Internet facility that links Web pages together, whether they exist on one server locally, or many servers around the world.

X25 A popular communications protocol used on WANs.

Index